Tragicomedy

Forms of Drama

Forms of Drama meets the need for accessible, mid-length volumes that offer undergraduate readers authoritative guides to the distinct forms of global drama. From classical Greek tragedy to Chinese pear garden theatre, cabaret to *kathakali*, the series equips readers with models and methodologies for analysing a wide range of performance practices and engaging with these as 'craft'.

SERIES EDITOR: SIMON SHEPHERD

Cabaret
978-1-3501-4025-7
William Grange

Pageant
978-1-3501-4451-4
Joan FitzPatrick Dean

Satire
978-1-3501-4007-3
Joel Schechter

Tragicomedy
978-1-3501-4430-9
Brean Hammond

Tragicomedy

Brean Hammond

methuen | drama
LONDON • NEW YORK • OXFORD • NEW DELHI • SYDNEY

METHUEN DRAMA
Bloomsbury Publishing Plc
50 Bedford Square, London, WC1B 3DP, UK
1385 Broadway, New York, NY 10018, USA
29 Earlsfort Terrace, Dublin 2, Ireland

First published in Great Britain 2021

Series design by Charlotte Daniels

A catalogue record for this book is available from the British Library.

Library of Congress Control Number: 2021938162

ISBN: HB: 978-1-3501-4431-6
PB: 978-1-3501-4430-9
ePDF: 978-1-3501-4433-0
eBook: 978-1-3501-4432-3

Series: Forms of Drama

Typeset by Integra Software Services Pvt. Ltd.
Printed and bound in Great Britain

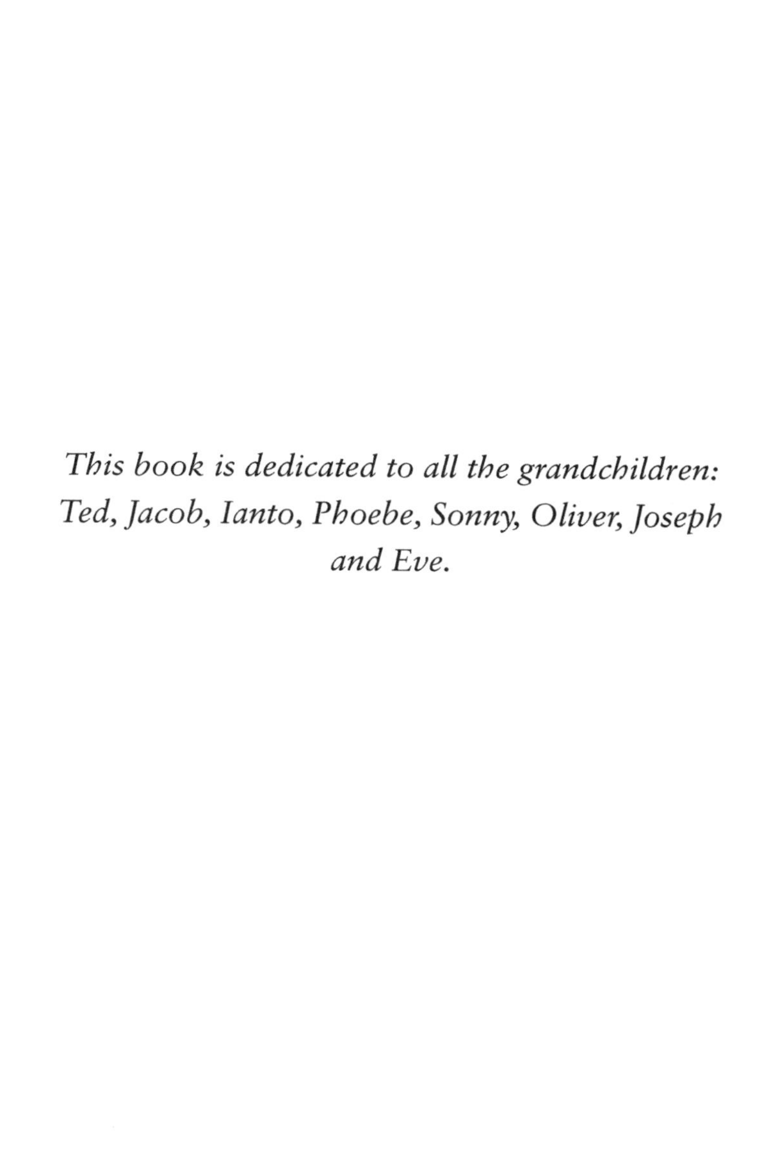

This book is dedicated to all the grandchildren: Ted, Jacob, Ianto, Phoebe, Sonny, Oliver, Joseph and Eve.

CONTENTS

ILLUSTRATIONS

SERIES PREFACE

The scope of this series is scripted aesthetic activity that works by means of personation.

Scripting is done in a wide variety of ways. It may, most obviously, be the more or less detailed written text familiar in the stage play of the western tradition, which not only provides lines to be spoken but directions for speaking them. Or it may be a set of instructions, a structure or scenario, on the basis of which performers improvise, drawing, as they do so, on an already learnt repertoire of routines and responses. Or there may be nothing written, just sets of rules, arrangements and even speeches orally handed down over time. The effectiveness of such unwritten scripting can be seen in the behaviour of audiences, who, without reading a script, have learnt how to conduct themselves appropriately at the different activities they attend. For one of the key things that unwritten script specifies and assumes is the relationship between the various groups of participants, including the separation, or not, between doers and watchers.

What is scripted is specifically an aesthetic activity. That specification distinguishes drama from non-aesthetic activity using personation. Following the work of Erving Goffman in the mid-1950s, especially his book *The Presentation of Self in Everyday Life*, the social sciences have made us richly aware of the various ways in which human interactions are performed. Going shopping, for example, is a performance in that we present a version of ourselves in each encounter we make. We may indeed have changed our clothes before setting out. This, though, is a social performance.

The distinction between social performance and aesthetic activity is not clear-cut. The two sorts of practice overlap and mingle with one another. An activity may be more or less aesthetic, but the crucial distinguishing feature is the status of the aesthetic element. Going shopping may contain an aesthetic element – decisions about clothes and shoes to wear – but its purpose is not deliberately to make an aesthetic activity or to mark itself as different from everyday social life. The aesthetic element is not regarded as a general requirement. By contrast a court-room trial may be seen as a social performance, in that it has an important social function, but it is at the same time extensively scripted, with prepared speeches, costumes and choreography. This scripted aesthetic element assists the social function in that it conveys a sense of more than everyday importance and authority to proceedings which can have life-changing impact. Unlike the activity of going shopping the aesthetic element here is not optional. Derived from tradition it is a required component that gives the specific identity to the activity.

It is defined as an activity in that, in a way different from a painting of Rembrandt's mother or a statue of Ramesses II, something is made to happen over time. And, unlike a symphony concert or firework display, that activity works by means of personation. Such personation may be done by imitating and interpreting – 'inhabiting' – other human beings, fictional or historical, and it may use the bodies of human performers or puppets. But it may also be done by a performer who produces a version of their own self, such as a stand-up comedian or court official on duty, or by a performer who, through doing the event, acquires a self with special status as with the *hijras* securing their sacredness by doing the ritual practice of *badhai*.

Some people prefer to call many of these sorts of scripted aesthetic events not drama but cultural performance. But there are problems with this. First, such labelling tends to keep in place an old-fashioned idea of western scholarship that drama, with its origins in ancient Greece, is a specifically European 'high' art. Everything outside it is then potentially, and damagingly, consigned to a domain which may be neither 'art' nor 'high'. Instead the European stage play and its like can best be regarded as a subset of the general category, distinct from the rest in that two groups of people come together in order specifically to present and watch a story being acted out by imitating other persons and settings. Thus the performance of a stage play in this tradition consists of two levels of activity using personation: the interaction of audience and performers and the interaction between characters in a fictional story.

The second problem with the category of cultural performance is that it downplays the significance and persistence of script, in all its varieties. With its roots in the traditional behaviours and beliefs of a society, script gives specific instructions for the form – the materials, the structure and sequence – of the aesthetic activity, the drama. So too, as we have noted, script defines the relationships between those who are present in different capacities at the event.

It is only by attending to what is scripted, to the form of the drama, that we can best analyse its functions and pleasures. At its most simple, analysis of form enables us to distinguish between different sorts of aesthetic activity. The masks used in *kathakali* look different from those used in *commedia dell'arte*. They are made of different materials, designs and colours. The roots of those differences lie in their separate cultural traditions and systems of living. For similar reasons the puppets of *karagoz* and *wayang* differ. But perhaps more importantly the attention to form provides a basis for exploring the operation and effects of a particular work. Those who regularly participate in and watch drama, of whatever sort, learn to recognize and remember the forms of what they see and hear. When one drama has family resemblances to another, in its organization and use of materials, structure and sequences, those who attend it develop expectations as to how it will – or indeed should – operate. It then becomes possible to specify how a particular work subverts, challenges or enhances these expectations.

Expectation doesn't only govern response to individual works, however. It can shape, indeed has shaped, assumptions about which dramas are worth studying. It is well established that Asia has ancient and rich dramatic traditions, from the Indian sub-continent to Japan, as does Europe, and these are studied with enthusiasm. But there is much less widespread activity, at least in western universities, in relation to the traditions of, say, Africa, Latin America and the Middle East. Secondly, even within the recognized traditions, there are assumptions that some dramas are more 'artistic', or indeed more 'serious', 'higher' even, than others. Thus it may be assumed that *noh* or classical tragedy will require the sort of close attention to craft which is not necessary for mumming or *badhai*.

Both sets of assumptions here keep in place a system which allocates value. This series aims to counteract a discriminatory value system by ranging as widely as possible across world practices and by giving the same sort of attention to all the forms it features. Thus book-length studies of forms such as *al-halqa*, *hana keaka* and *ta'zieh* will appear in English for perhaps the first time. Those studies, just like those of *kathakali*, tragicomedy and the rest, will adopt the same basic approach. That approach consists of an historical overview of the development of a form combined with, indeed anchored in, detailed analysis of examples and case studies. One of the benefits of properly detailed analysis is that it can reveal the construction which gives a work the appearance of being serious, artistic, and indeed 'high'.

What does that work of construction is script. This series is grounded in the idea that all forms of drama have script of some kind and that an understanding of drama, of any sort, has to include analysis of that script. In taking this approach, books in this series again challenge an assumption which has in recent times governed the study of drama. Deriving from the supposed, but artificial, distinction between cultural performance and drama, many accounts of cultural performance ignore its scriptedness and assume that the proper way of studying it is simply to describe how its practitioners behave and what they make. This is useful enough, but to leave it at that is to produce something that looks like a form of lesser anthropology. The description of behaviours is only the first step in that it establishes what the script is. The next step is to analyse how the script and form work and how they create effect.

But it goes further than this. The close-up analyses of materials, structures and sequences – of scripted forms – show how they emerge from and connect deeply back into the modes of life and belief to which they are necessary. They tell us in short why, in any culture, the drama needs to be done. Thus by adopting the extended model of drama, and by approaching all dramas in the same way, the books in this series aim to tell us why, in all societies, the activities of scripted aesthetic personation – dramas – keep happening, and need to keep happening.

I am grateful, as always, to Mick Wallis for helping me to think through these issues. Any clumsiness or stupidity is entirely my own.

Simon Shepherd

ACKNOWLEDGEMENTS

My main debts are to my 'reading team': Gerald Baker, Janette Dillon and Simon Shepherd; and to my 'modern languages team': Steve Hunt, Alessandra Legge, Wendy Perkins and Tatiana Supron. I have had invaluable assistance along the way from Joseph Anderton, Matt Buckley, Jonathan McAllister, Cynthia Marsh and Jim Moran.

Much of this book was written during the period of Covid-19 lockdown. Owing to library closures, it has not always been possible to consult authoritative scholarly editions. I have relied upon electronic resources and those in my own personal collection more than is ideal. The result, as far as citation is concerned, is a little uneven, but I hope that this does not detract too much from the reading experience.

Introduction

The Origins and Nature of Tragicomedy

Genre theorists have long abandoned the idea that a genre can be boiled down to a set of prescriptions, because exception after exception simply eclipses the rule. For the most part, genres are not *invented*. No one sits down and thinks them up. As Alastair Fowler argued, genres are more adequately described by the concept of 'family resemblance' modified in the direction of genetics:

> In literature, the basis of resemblance lies in literary tradition. What produces generic resemblances ... is tradition: a sequence of influence and imitation and inherited codes connecting works in the genre. As kinship makes a family, so literary relations of this sort form a genre. (Fowler 1985: 42)

Here, the idea might be that, on an analogy with natural selection though with more intentionality than is usually attributed to nature, a writer adds something to an existing form and because it is successful – it works, readers and spectators like it – others copy it. Thus the new feature, even if accidentally conceived, becomes part of the form. It helps to create the horizon of expectation that subsequent consumers of the literary or dramatic type bring to their reception of it.

Tragicomedy gets closer to the 'invention' end of the spectrum than do most other genres. English tragicomedy is unusual in that its formation, though certainly not out of nothing, was largely monogenetic – brought about by particular writers. Those writers in on the ground floor in England include John Marston (1576–1634), John Fletcher (1579–1625), Francis Beaumont (1584–1616) and William Shakespeare (1564–1616). Ben Jonson (1572–1637) did not write tragicomedy, but he was important in conferring respectability upon the work of those who did. This group of writers created in the space of two decades a newly mixed, newly blended species of theatrical writing that, in the decades leading to the closure of the theatres in 1642, achieved 'brand recognition'. Theatregoers could recognize many of the dramatic elements that went into the making of such a play and readers who picked up a playbook that was called a 'tragicomedy' on its title page had a good idea of what they were about to receive.

If he were writing today, Fowler might have been attracted to the Richard Dawkins-inspired language of memes. 'Meme' is defined in the *Oxford English Dictionary* as 'a cultural element or behavioural trait whose transmission and consequent persistence in a population, although occurring by non-genetic means (esp. imitation), is considered as analogous to the inheritance of a gene'. Ideas and cultural elements can evolve and replicate; genre formation might be considered the result of such memetic transmission, a process to which individual creativity contributes in a more major way, in the case of tragicomedy, than in the case of most literary and dramatic genres. In tragicomedy, memes already familiar from heterogeneous sources – romance, classical myth, folk tale, prose fiction, jestbooks and 'coney-catching' pamphlets and earlier plays – are assembled in such a way as to give an increasingly recognizable and theatrically desirable structure to the whole play. Readers of this book will become familiar with tragicomic memes, but one or two examples might help at this introductory point. Characters with uncertain parentage, especially female characters whose virtue appears to transcend their station in life, will give audiences the idea that social status is more fluid in such plays than it is in tragedy or comedy. Variations on the theme of 'resurrection' will enable dramatists to fulfil the agenda, defined below in the section 'Tragicomedy's English development' by Shakespeare's writing partner John Fletcher, of bringing characters near to death – even persuading audiences that they are actually dead – while reserving them for a happy ending. Various 'protector' figures provide audiences with early insurance against worst-case scenarios, assurances that the worst possible consequences of human action will not transpire as they will do in tragedy. These ideas – devices, memes – recur.

European Beginnings

The Italian Renaissance is the seedbed of much European theatre. Although the country's fragmented political and linguistic nature, and its long-lasting occupation by foreign powers, prevented it from amassing a significant body of dramatic literature written in a national language, Italians made an enormous contribution to scenic design, theatre construction and the art of acting. Lacking a cultural capital boasting a commercial theatre institution, Italy's itinerant *commedia dell'arte* was nevertheless widely influential. Tragicomedy itself is more the province of the *commedia erudita*, however: dramatic writing and theorizing produced by the educated elite. In the devising of new forms and in thinking and theorizing about such forms, Italy was in the forefront of dramaturgical discussion. Humanist scholarship disseminated through print resulted in editions of Roman dramatists – Terence in 1470 and Plautus in 1472 – and of classical thinking on dramatic structure and composition through Aristotle's *Poetics* and Horace's *Ars Poetica*. Pastoral tragicomedy was first devised in Italy as far back as 1480, with Poliziano's *Orfeo*, the two enduring examples being Tasso's *Aminta* (1573) and Guarini's *Il Pastor Fido* (1590), about which we will have much more to say because it had a direct influence on English development of the form.

In the early seventeenth century, at virtually the same time as John Fletcher was theorizing tragicomedy in England (see further the section 'Tragicomedy's English Development' and Chapter 1), in Spain the astonishingly prolific Lope de Vega was establishing the three-act *comedia* as the most favoured form of Spanish drama in the commercial theatre. Lope Félix de Vega Carpio (1562–1635) lived a life that would have done justice to a tragicomic adventure plot. Apparently he could compose verse before he could write. Probably university-educated though the son of a craftsman, he sailed with the Armada, was secretary to two great noblemen, was married twice, had scandalous affairs with actresses, took holy orders in 1614 and claimed to have written 1,500 plays. Modern scholarship accepts his authorship of more than 300 of the 500 plays attributed to him that have survived. Spain had had commercial theatres and companies of paid actors since the middle of the sixteenth century. Despite continuing Jesuit opposition to institutional theatre parallel to Puritan outrage in England, permanent public theatres known as *corrales* became a feature of all major cities. The fare devised for such buildings by Lope de Vega was verse comedy in varying rhyme schemes. Although Lope does not refer to his work as tragicomedy, it did not observe strict generic separation. In 1609, just before Fletcher, Lope defended the mixed mode in *Arte nuevo de hacer comedias en este tiempo* ('The new art of making comedies in this time'):

> Lo trágico y lo cómico mezclado,
> y Terencio con Séneca, aunque sea
> como otro Minotauro de Pasife,
> harán grave una parte, otra ridícula,

> que aquesta variedad deleita mucho:
> buen ejemplo nos da naturaleza,
> que por tal variedad tiene belleza. (ll. 174–80)
>
> (The tragic and the comic mingled, both Terence and Seneca together, although it may seem like some other Minotaur, born of Pasiphae [i.e. a strange hybrid], this will make it in one respect serious and in another absurd, since this mixture offers much delight; Nature shows us this example, since through such diversity it possesses true beauty.)

This emphasis on combining Terence with Seneca, the grave and the ridiculous, reflects the diverse sources from which Spanish *comedia* took its plots: Spanish history, legends and ballads, saints' lives, biblical stories and the Italian *novelle* so exhaustively mined by English dramatists also.

In France at the close of the sixteenth century, a company arrived at the Hôtel de Bourgogne (Paris' only theatre) that had as its dramatist Alexandre Hardy (*c.*1575–*c.*1632), the first French professional playwright, who devised pastorals, plays borrowed from Spanish models and, importantly for us, tragicomedies. Between 1623 and 1628, thirty-four of his many hundreds of compositions were published, several of those being tragicomedies. They were still being performed at the Hôtel de Bourgogne in the 1630s, a decade in which active patronage of theatre from Richelieu transformed the theatrical scene. While at the Bourgogne a company called the 'Comédiens du Roi' was performing, Richelieu encouraged the foundation of a rival theatre at the Marais, in a converted tennis court tenanted by Montdory and his formerly itinerant troupe. Paris now had a duopoly rather like London post-1660. Richelieu lent his direct encouragement to write plays to a group of five dramatists, including Mairet, Rotrou and Corneille. Tragicomedies continued to be a popular mode, until Corneille rocked the boat with *Le Cid* (1637), a story more fully told in Chapter 3 of this book.

Tragicomedy's English Development

Influenced by Horace's passage on 'satyr drama' in his *Ars Poetica* 220–33 and by Italian theorists Antonio Minturno (1500–74) and Giovanni Battista Guarini (1538–1612), John Marston wrote a play called *The Malcontent* that was recorded in the Stationers' Register on 5 July 1604 as 'an Enterlude called the *Malecontent Tragiecomedia*'. Even before the booksellers Aspley and Thorpe recorded Marston's play as their property under this generic label, there is evidence of some generic confusion: stirrings and uncertainties. In 1575, for example, the title page of George Gascoigne's *The Glasse of Governement* is called 'A tragicall Comedie so entituled, bycause therein are handled as well the rewardes for Vertues, as also the punishment for Vices'. In this understanding, a play becomes a tragicomedy if some of its characters prosper while others don't – which happens in pretty much every play you can think of. A decade later, John Lyly's play *Campaspe* (1584) is termed a 'tragicall Comedie of Alexander and Campaspe' in the running title. Actually it would be difficult to find a more comic comedy than *Campaspe*, in which love so easily finds a way. Alexander the Great willingly relinquishes his love Campaspe to the painter Apelles, having learned that he can conquer the world but he cannot command love where it isn't requited. Many tyrants in later actual tragicomedies will not see things this way.

Difficulties with the generic ascription are never wholly absent. *The Witch of Edmonton*, a collaborative play by Rowley, Dekker and Ford published in 1621, was called a 'tragi-comedy' on its 1658 quarto title page, but the play does not end well. Although the wicked characters Mother Sawyer the witch and Frank and Winnifride repent, they are not reprieved and the play's final line is as far away as possible from the spirit of tragicomedy as this book will define it: 'Harms past may be lamented, not redeemed' (Rowley, Dekker and Ford 1986: 5.3.172). Unsurprisingly, Charles Gildon reclassified this as a tragedy in his 1699 *Lives and Characters of the English Dramatick Poets*. In the 1603 Quarto of *Hamlet*, uncertainty resulting from generic mixing has become a joke. Corambis (the Polonius figure in the 'bad' or short first quarto) introduces the players thus:

> The best actors in Christendom, either for comedy, tragedy, history, pastoral, pastoral-historical, historical-comical, comical-historical-pastoral, tragedy-historical ... (Shakespeare 2007: 7.295–8)

By then, as this book argues, Shakespeare has already had the first significant achievement in tragicomedy with *Much Ado About Nothing* (1598).

By 1610, we have our first English attempt to theorize this new kind of play. John Fletcher attempted to provide guidance when introducing his readers to a play, *The Faithful Shepherdess* (1610), that had been widely misunderstood in performance:

> It is a pastorall Tragie-comedie ... A tragie-comedie is not so called in respect of mirth and killing, but in respect it wants deaths, which is inough to make it no tragedie, yet brings some neere it, which is inough to make it no comedie: which must be a representation of familiar people, with such kinde of trouble as no life be questiond, so that a God is as lawfull in this as in a tragedie, and meane people as in a comedie. Thus much I hope will serue to iustifie my Poem, and make you vnderstand it, to teach you more for nothing, I do not know that I am in conscience bound. (Beaumont and Fletcher 1976: vol. 3, 497, ll. 3, 20–8)

Here, Fletcher defines tragicomedy as a kind of playwriting that brings characters to the graveside but doesn't kick them into the hole. The syntax is far from lucid, but I would construe the third 'which' clause to mean that characters in comedy must be 'familiar people'. And whatever difficulties they face do not bring their very existence into question.

They run into trouble but not into mortal danger ('as no life be questiond'). Tragicomedy, being a mixed form, can have Gods *and* 'meane people' in it. This is its real value. Fletcher would seem to be providing more room for the imagination than the classical genres offered and appears to challenge the apartheid that separates the nobility from common folks in the prescriptions for playwriting that prevail, particularly those found in Aristotle's *Poetics*. By 1616, the folio edition of Ben Jonson's *Works* has a title page in which the figure of Tragicomoedia stands atop the façade of a Renaissance building, flanked by emblematic figures entitled 'Satvr' and 'Pastor' (see Figure 1). This suggests that Jonson thought of Jacobean tragicomedy as a form colonized either by satire, as in the case of Marston and possibly Jonson himself, or by pastoral, as in the case of Beaumont, Fletcher and Shakespeare. It was in the latter form, that of pastoral tragicomedy, that it would have a future. The first chapter of the present book analyses the new mode that the Fletcher coterie had introduced, following that with two chapters exploring tragicomedy's development over the next century and a half until the generic descriptor falls out of use. The book's final chapter considers a case for melodrama as a cutting from tragicomic stock and goes on to analyse three particular cases of late-nineteenth- to twentieth-century tragicomedy, after the genre's sequential history is over, but where it has been revived for particular reasons.

Can we offer some account of what space tragicomedy occupied in the repertoire as a whole? Are there facts and figures that can give the genre presence? In *Lost Plays in Shakespeare's England*, David McInnis and Matthew Steggle write that 'in the lifetime of the commercial playhouses, roughly 1567 to 1642, around 3000 different plays must have been written and staged in them: of these, a minority survive … The latest and most authoritative count puts the number of surviving plays at 543' (McInnis and Steggle 2014: 1–2). We are aware in addition of some 744 plays that do not survive other than by mention of their titles. Of those 543 extant plays, Gerald

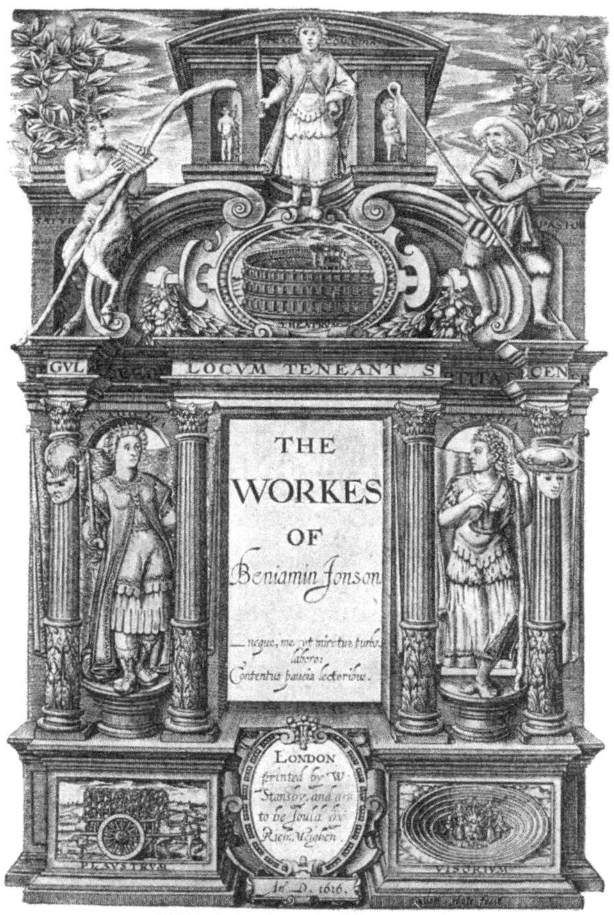

TITLE-PAGE OF BEN JONSON'S WORKS, 1616.

Figure 1 *The frontispiece illustration to the 1616 edition of Ben Jonson's* Workes. *The figures of Satvr and Pastor, representing satirical and pastoral forms of art, are positioned in the pediment of a Renaissance building, with Tragicomoedia standing above and between them, wearing comic apparel but holding the crown and sceptre of tragedy. Photo by Culture Club/Getty Images.*

Baker and I have calculated that some 150 were tragicomedies, roughly 28 per cent of the entire surviving repertoire.[1]

How is this figure computed? Some of the plays featured in this count were not called tragicomedies at the time of their performance, but most of them were so called before the end of the seventeenth century. As in the case of Marston's *Malcontent*, plays can be designated 'tragicomedies' when entered in the Stationers' Register. 'A play booke beinge a Tragecomedye called, The Noble man written by Cyrill Tourneur' was entered in 1612, though this play does not survive. The first title page I have been able to find is that for the octavo edition of Samuel Daniel's *Hymen's Triumph* (1615), followed in 1623 by *The Deuils Law-case, or, When Women goe to Law, the Deuill is full of Businesse: A new Tragecomoedy* by John Webster. In the Bodleian Library, there exists a transcript of Middleton's play *The Witch* in the hand of the scribe Ralph Crane (MS Malone 12). Although undated, bibliographic evidence dates this manuscript to 1625. On the title page, the play is called 'A Tragi-Coomedie'. Even where a generic ascription is not made on a title page, paratexts (features such as prefaces, dedications and commendatory verses that frame the text itself) occasionally give us clues. Thomas Heywood, in the 1624 quarto of his play *The English Traveller*, writes an address 'To the Reader' which describes it as a 'Tragi-Comedy', asserts that he has had a hand, 'or at the least a maine finger' in some 220 plays, and gives us reasons why his plays have never come out in handsome volumes called 'Workes', implying a comparison with Jonson and Shakespeare: 'it never was any great ambition in me, to bee in this kind Voluminiously read' is his surprisingly frank comment (A3f).

Philip Massinger (1583–1640) was a playwright whose *oeuvre* was crucial to the continuing success of tragicomedy into the 1630s, ensuring the popularity of the genre to the extent that in the years 1635–7, some thirty new tragicomedies were produced. All of Massinger's major tragicomedies, *The Renegado*, *The Picture*, *The Maid of Honour* and *The Emperour of the East*, were published between 1630 and 1632 in quarto format and are called 'tragaecomoedies' on their title pages. All bar *The Renegado* have that generic message reinforced by commendatory verses attached, by Aston Cokayne (and Thomas Jay in the case of *The Picture*) in which the plays are again termed 'Tragaecomaedies'. When the copyright to *The Picture* was sold on by Thomas Walkeley to John Waterson in 1634, Waterson bought 'all his estate right Title & interest in a Tragi-Comedy called the Picture written by Mr Messinger' (Edwards and Gibson 1976: vol. 3, 185). These early examples show that Massinger was a recognized master of tragicomedy, suggesting a gradually increasing recognition factor for that generic designation, to the extent that it even found its way into legal documents.

Classification of plays does not begin in earnest, however, until booksellers such as Francis Kirkman begin to see its utility in leading customers to what they might want to buy. In 1661, Kirkman advertised *A true, perfect, and exact catalogue of all the comedies, tragedies, tragi-comedies, pastorals, masques and interludes, that were ever yet printed and published, till this present year 1661*, supplying details of all the booksellers' shops where they could be bought. Extended in 1671, Kirkman's catalogue was the first to include tragicomedies and to identify plays by that designation. Commercial interests were making themselves felt, so that when the second folio collection of the plays of Beaumont and Fletcher was published in 1679 as *Fifty comedies and tragedies written by Francis Beaumont and John Fletcher, Gentlemen*, several of the plays are identified as tragicomedies on the title pages. Other catalogues followed Kirkman, but the most industrious cataloguer of plays and the individual who provides the best understanding of how seventeenth-century theatregoers thought of plays was Gerard Langbaine (1656–92). Trading on his acquaintance with Kirkman, Langbaine assembled a personal collection of nearly a thousand playbooks. This led him to compile, from 1680 onwards, a series of increasingly sophisticated catalogues that are, as Paulina Kewes's *Oxford Dictionary of National Biography* (*ODNB*) entry says, 'a landmark in the history of dramatic authorship, bibliography, source study, and criticism'.[2] Langbaine is first to describe Shakespeare's *The Winter's Tale* as a tragicomedy in his 1691 *An Account of the English Dramatick Poets*; and he makes some interesting ascriptions, such as calling *The Merchant of Venice* a tragicomedy in his *A New Catalogue of English Plays* (1688), better known under its spurious title *Momus triumphans, or, The Plagiaries of the English Stage*. That would repay further investigation. Although Langbaine's classifications are retrospective, it is reasonable to assume that he was drawing on the collective wisdom of audiences, readers and booksellers over a long period.

The Purpose of Tragicomedy

An introduction needs to consider briefly why tragicomedy arose. What was it for? What appetites did it satisfy? What could it achieve that, separately, tragedy and comedy could not? This conversation begins, as so many do, with the *Poetics*, a general account of tragedy drawing on the actual tragedies written and performed in Greece in the fifth century BCE. The treatise attributed to Aristotle (but now suspected to include contributions from the Athenian Academy) allows for the possibility that tragedies might end *happily*: '[Discovery] ... will arouse either pity or fear ... and it will also serve to bring about the happy or unhappy ending' (*Poetics* 2.11, 1453a30–9; Nevitt and Pollard 2019: 23). Although Aristotle does not use the term 'tragicomedy', he creates the space that later tragicomic theory and practice will occupy. What is that space?

Let's briefly revisit the final line of *The Witch of Edmonton*, 'Harms past may be lamented, not redeemed'. Tragicomedy's primary purpose in the early modern period is to redeem 'harms past'. If tragedy deals with inevitable experience, if, as the sleepwalking Lady Macbeth says 'What's done, cannot be undone', then the point of tragicomedy is precisely to undo what has been done. Its memes are structured so as to offer its characters an opportunity for a second chance, whereby the harms they have done during their first journey through life can be mitigated, even if never quite entirely removed. Tragicomic art offers the possibility of atonement, not frequently afforded by life itself and not offered by tragedy. Tyrannical rulers who are also husbands and fathers make catastrophic misjudgements that put their nearest and dearest in jeopardy. For those errors to be redeemed, realization followed by repentance, and atonement enabled by grace, are the mechanisms that need to be sprung. Particularly in the work of Shakespeare, those developments are quasi-religious, engaging procedures that bring to mind those of the Christian religion – importantly, resurrection. The return of seemingly lost children is a recurrent meme in tragicomedy, effecting a process of patrilinear repair – the suturing up of a wounded bloodline. Explicitly stated in *Winter's Tale* but implied in all early modern tragicomedy is a form of time reversal. Time has to be halted, its ravages upon human destinies stopped in their tracks. Where that becomes a possibility, so does the operation of magic and the presence of gods upon the earth. In typical tragicomedies the characters are struck by a particular congeries of feeling – awe or wonder. If Aristotle was correct to associate tragedy with pity and fear, the signature emotions of tragicomedy are awe and wonder.

The comic side of the tragicomic contract is fulfilled by spectacle and special effects not acceptable in comedy itself where plausibility and social realism have a stronger hold. But tragicomedy does borrow the promiscuous mingling of persons of differing social ranks that Aristotle precluded. Socially elevated characters find themselves sharing the company of ne'er-do-wells and zanies such as Autolycus in *Winter's Tale* and the pox-crazed Lieutenant in Fletcher's smash-hit tragicomedy of *c.*1619, *The Humorous Lieutenant*. Not only do the nobles breathe their air but they interact with them in plot terms. The meme of the displaced princess, Perdita in *Winter's Tale* or Celia in *Humorous Lieutenant*, provides roles for feisty females who can speak truth to power, witness Perdita's holding her own on the subject of artificial cultivars in plant husbandry and Celia's plain speaking when the aged King Antigonus shows his intention of making her his mistress. As this book argues, tragicomedy began to develop its own distinctive dramaturgical format, that of the blended scene, where the writer tries to develop an amalgam that will wrong-foot the spectator to the extent that s/he is not absolutely sure how to react. The perfectly blended tragicomic tonality, the tragicomic moment, is one of its major legacies to twentieth-century practitioners of the form.

Nineteenth- and Twentieth-century Tragicomedy

Tragicomedy's hold on the theatrical imagination waned in the eighteenth century, a story told in Chapter 3 of this book. What had become its structure, the 'double plot' where the serious high plot dealt with aristocratic love-*versus*-honour dilemmas while the secondary comic plot concerned itself with the marital/sexual exploits of characters lower down the pecking order, made it vulnerable to criticism on the grounds of politeness and plausibility. Such characters and such content did not strike a chord with an increasingly middle-class audience demanding to see representations of people like themselves engaged in social problems, with plots that might help them to understand how society and its individual members ticked. Tragicomedy broke apart, its high plot diverted into stiff-necked stories of heroes from ancient, classical or early history – now forgotten plays such as Samuel Madden's *Themistocles, the Lover of his Country* (1729), set in the post-Salamis phase of the Greco-Persian Wars, or James Thomson's Roman play *Sophonisba* (1730), with its oft-parodied line 'O Sophonisba! Sophonisba o!' – while increasingly sentimentalized versions of the comic plot eventually made for a situation in which laughter itself became bad form and 'laughing comedies' had to be reinvented by Goldsmith and Sheridan.

Chapter 4 begins with a section devoted to the possibility that some of the satisfactions of older tragicomedy resurfaced in nineteenth-century melodrama. This is a speculative argument, but one that I think is worth considering. Although since the late nineteenth century the label has had occasional outings, there is no continuous generic history in the nineteenth and twentieth centuries. When later dramatists have taken it up, they have done so because particular plays that they have written are not conceived or adequately described in traditional generic terms. The final chapter therefore considers under the aspect of tragicomedy some individual examples, Ibsen's *The Wild Duck* (1884), Chekhov's *The Cherry Orchard* (1904) and Beckett's *Waiting for Godot* (1953), outlining the conditions that give 'tragicomedy' explanatory force in each case. For Ibsen, the form exploits the divergence between the aspirations of individuals and the social compromises that render ideals hypocritical. Chekhov's experiment is to find a blended tone that articulates the disorientation of an entire social group, a group that no longer knows what it should think or how it should feel. Beckett designs linguistic forms that express the predicament of human existence as it is left by the horrors of global war and catastrophe.

As I write this, Covid-19 has halted the production of the National Theatre's revival of one of the most remarkable tragicomedies ever written, Friedrich Dürrenmatt's 1956 play *The Visit: A Tragi-comedy.* First published as *Der Besuch der Alten Dame* (*The Visit of the Old Lady*), it was translated by Patrick Bowles for a Grove Press edition in 1962. The National's version is an adaptation by Tony Kushner, based on an English translation by Maurice Valency, that transfers the action from a nowhere town called Guellen in Central Europe to a nowhere town called Slurry in New York state.

I will conclude this Introduction with a brief discussion of the play in Bowles's translation, as my way of speaking back to the infection that silenced the play, and because the National Theatre's high-profile production, directed by Jeremy Herrin and starring Lesley Manville and Hugo Weaving, proves the continuing relevance of that play and of writing in the tragicomic mode. Chapter 4 sheds more light on how Dürrenmatt was able to conceive this ingenious parable of revenge and justice, through the analysis of some distinguished earlier examples of tragicomic art.

The play is set in a small, failing town somewhere in Central Europe called Guellen. This dumpy little place is to be distinguished by a visit from the richest woman in the world, Claire Zachanassian, born and raised in Guellen as Claire Wascher. The town's officials are looking to her childhood sweetheart, the now 65-year-old grocer Alfred Ill (the name even in the original German is 'ill', as in 'sick', but it is difficult to reproduce typographically), to woo her into making a huge bequest to revive the town. There are two *coups de théâtre*. In Act 1, Claire agrees to provide a huge sum of money for urban regeneration and for gifts to individuals, but only if the town agrees to the judicial execution of Ill. (Ill, it turns out, got her pregnant and then bribed two witnesses to deny his paternity before a crooked magistrate, so that he could marry a wealthier woman. Claire, forced into prostitution, met her oil billionaire in a brothel.) In Act 2, it is revealed that Claire herself is responsible for Guellen's ruin. She has bought up and closed down all the local industry. Although the upright Guelleners protest that they will never hand Ill over, it is apparent throughout Act 2 that they are living vastly above their means on credit, presumably expecting to pay their debts on a future date … when they come into money. There are clear signs that public opinion is turning against Ill, figured in the new yellow shoes that all the Guelleners are mysteriously sporting. By the end of Act 2, Ill tries desperately to leave the town but, although the citizens do not prevent him, he finds that he simply cannot get on the train. In Act 3, he is convicted after a show trial in which the citizens trump up noble reasons for their actions and the world's press misreports the entire event. Ill is killed in a balletic mime, and a Greek-style chorus of Guelleners remains to celebrate Zachanassian and the town's prosperity.

In a postscript, Dürrenmatt wrote that 'nothing could harm this comedy with a tragic end more than heavy seriousness' (Dürrenmatt 1962: 108). This resonates with later tragicomic aperçus: Nell's remark in Samuel Beckett's *Endgame*, 'Nothing is funnier than unhappiness' (Beckett [1958] 1973: 20), and a statement made by Harold Pinter, 'The thing about tragedy is that it's funny, and then it's no longer funny'. Ill's death, Dürrenmatt says, is 'both meaningful and meaningless' (Dürrenmatt 1962: 107). The greatest difference between this play and the examples of tragicomedy considered in Chapters 1 and 2 is that no concept of divinity or even providence presides over its dramatic world. No morality prevails. The Guelleners who profit by Ill's death are no more moral, no better than he is. Any happy ending is powerfully undercut by the cynicism and cruelty of Ill's sacrifice. Also, much of the play is funny. From the gaffes and blunders committed by a nowhere place putting on a show for a visitor entirely out of its league – the upstaging of the choir by an express train, the sign-painter's misspelling and non-completion of Zachanassian's name – to the Schoolmaster's final act oration persuading the people that Ill's murder is an expression of an ideal, the action has the audience on the edge of uncomfortable laughter. What all of this suggests is that the matrix of tragicomedy is now comedy – that, up to a point, recent tragicomedies should strike the audience as funny. This is comedy, though, of a bleak pessimistic kidney, grotesque and black. Claire is travelling with a coffin that gains floral accretions as the play goes on. Before she declares her purpose, she makes a series of dark allusions to the death penalty, death by strangling and so forth. Although once a flame-haired beauty, she is now a parody of her younger self. That she plans to put Alfred Ill in the coffin does not preclude a romantic scene as the couple visit old haunts and reminisce. Eros and Thanatos are spine-chillingly juxtaposed.

The Visit's ending, in which an individual is sacrificed for the sake of a society's overall prosperity, is pitting the customary social objectives of comedy in direct opposition to the individualistic objectives of tragedy. Dürrenmatt's postscript denies any connection with Surrealism, discouraging allegorical readings: 'Claire Zachanassian doesn't represent Justice or the Marshall Plan or even the Apocalypse, she's purely and simply what she is, namely, the richest woman in the world' (106). The selfsame sentence, though, compares her to the Greek Medea and speaks of her 'moving outside the human pale', a 'stone idol' (106–7). Male actors embody trees and nature; and the presence in the cast list of a group of characters called Toby, Roby, Koby and Loby – the latter a pair of blind and castrated twins, who turn out to be the witnesses against Claire, tracked down and maimed by her – does not suggest an entirely realist play. And the Schoolmaster tells Ill that 'I know one day an old lady will come for us too, and then what happened to you will happen to us' (77). Like *Waiting for Godot*, the play is what we might call 'allegorogenic': it generates possibilities for allegory. Personally, I find it difficult to resist the idea that the play figures the rise of Nazism, depicting as it does capitalist and patriotic interests combining to undermine a community's values and corrode its culture (as the Mayor says: 'a city of Humanist traditions. Goethe spent a night here. Brahms composed a quartet here' [53]), until it agrees to scapegoat and murder one of its citizens – a sick citizen called 'Ill', is he perhaps a Jew? The ubiquitous yellow boots would then be a symbol in reverse of the yellow star that all Jews were forced by the Nazis to wear? Possibly Ill cannot leave town because he has internalized the shame and disgrace of being a scapegoat, as, sadly, some Jews actually did? You can go a long way with this allegory, but not all the way.

This book tells the story of how a tragicomedy such as *The Visit* could come to be written. The final chapter suggests that post-Second World War tragicomedy gains force from the horrific events of war and from the crisis that affects tragic drama in being adequate to represent such events. In a world that is meaningless and meaningful in equal measure, black and grotesque comedy, calling to mind the ironic 'horrid laughter' of Renaissance 'malcontent' tragicomedies, offers a way forward.

1

Tragicomedy's Early Development

Aristotle's *Poetics* and Its Legacy

The *Poetics* has its own inbuilt biases. When it began to be discussed systematically, in Italy in the mid-sixteenth century, some European scholars and dramatists would argue that, although the great philosopher had codified the nature of tragedy, implicitly distinguishing it from comedy, he had not necessarily said the last word. Was Aristotle justified, for example, in his low opinion of the associated theatre arts that realize a playscript in performance? 'Spectacle ... is the least artistic of all the parts, and has least to do with the art of poetry. The tragic effect is quite possible without a public performance and actors' (2.6; Nevitt and Pollard 2019: 20–1). In nineteenth-century England, writers such as Coleridge, Lamb and Hazlitt would develop Aristotle's hostility to spectacle into an intense animus against performance. Their thinking resulted from concentration on Shakespeare, where the staged versions available to them in performance were usually very different from those that they could read in the study. From the reading, they constructed Shakespeare as the unparalleled 'genius', whose drama had such imaginative reach and lyric power that it could only be compromised by stage actualization. To take Shakespeare out of a reader's head is to subject his poetic masterpieces to tinsel and pasteboard travesty. Tragicomedies, on the other hand, imported aspects of court masques in the earliest phase of their English development, providing opportunities for music, dance and spectacular stage effects. Symbiosis of script and theatrical representation would become a vital aspect of their success.

Tragic plots, for Aristotle, were most effective when they demonstrated design and necessity rather than chance and coincidence (2.9). Tragicomic writers, on the other hand, would leave much to chance – indeed, they would celebrate its seemingly random effects, patterning plot coincidences in such a manner that they could appear to show the hand of Providence. For Aristotle, specific qualifications had to be met by any would-be tragic protagonist. Protagonists would need to be exceptional men, highly placed in society – because, if they were not, how could they be of interest to spectators? Whole communities, kingdoms indeed, should depend on their rise and fall. Humdrum lives, even going through extreme vicissitudes, were not of concern to audiences. Further, those socially exalted protagonists could not be evil. Evocation of pity is central to the objectives and effects of tragedy – and you can't pity someone evil. A tragedy can't show a bad man passing from misery to happiness, therefore. This is 'the most untragic that can be; it has no one of the requisites of Tragedy; it does not appeal either to the human feeling in us, or to our pity, or to our fears' (2.13; Nevitt and Pollard 2019: 24).

Tragicomedy was to do less than it might have – though not nothing – to weaken the hold of the aristocracy on dramatic form, but it had greater effect in undermining the Aristotelian prescription that the central figure had to be virtuous. Tragicomic practitioners, Shakespeare prominent amongst them, refused to swallow that prescription whole. Observing that, in life, wicked persons *did* often prosper, and more generally that individual human trajectories were subject to greater vicissitude and complication than is covered in an inevitable tragic fall, tragicomedians devised characters and plots that might do greater justice to such complexity. The idea that tragicomedies are 'realistic' does not stand up to much inspection if what is meant is that they devise more naturalistic conventions of staging than do tragedies or comedies. 'Realistic' is hardly a convincing descriptor for Shakespeare's late-career romantic tragicomedies in which gods descend from the heavens. There is more promise in the suggestion that they seek greater 'truth to' the roller-coaster experience that living one's life provides. It is this sense of life's *chiaroscuro* that the Scots poet William Drummond tries to capture when he writes, in his treatise on death entitled *A Cypresse Grove* (1623): 'Everie one commeth there [into this world] to act his part of this Tragicomedie called Life' (Drummond 1623: 73).

After 1548, when the Italian classical scholar Francesco Robortelli had made a Latin version of the *Poetics* available, systematic study of that seminal text got under way. Giovanni Battisti Giraldi, commonly called Cinzio (anglicized as Cinthio) in his *Discorso intorno al comporre delle comedie e delle tragedie* (1554), translated into English in 1555, dwells on the question of happy-ending tragedies and, in that context, points out that the Roman comic dramatist Plautus had written just such a 'mixed' play, entitled *Amphitruo* (now usually referred to in its Greek form *Amphitryon*). The gods Jupiter and Mercury come down to earth, the former impersonating the Theban general Amphitryon and the latter his slave Sosia, with raunchily hilarious consequences when the general's wife Alcmena gets in on the action. The play begins with a prologue in which Mercury addresses the audience:

> What's that? Are you disappointed
> To find it's a *tragedy*? Well, I can easily change it.
> I'm a god, after all. I can easily make it a comedy,
> And never alter a line ... Very well.
> I'll meet you half-way, and make it a *tragi-comedy.* (Plautus 1977: 230)

Plautus seems to be having a joke at Aristotle's expense here. Because there are gods, important mortals and a significant *slave* in the cast, the play cannot be a tragedy according to Aristotle. Aristotle prohibits the mingling of high- and low-caste people in what is properly termed a tragedy. Mercury outranks Aristotle, however, so, by divine *fiat*, he can simply *declare* the play a mongrel form to which he will give the label 'tragicomedy' – and hereby produces the first recorded example of the word.

Sidney and Guarini

English discussion of such matters begins with the first sustained work of literary criticism in that language, Sir Philip Sidney's *The Defence of Poesy*. Written around 1580, circulated in manuscript but not printed until 1595, Sidney criticizes contemporary dramatists for not observing Aristotle's rules about time and place – even though 'unity' of place was not actually required by Aristotle but inferred by the Italian scholar Lodovico Castelvetro in the commentary to his 1570 translation of the *Poetics*, with which Sidney was probably familiar. Failure to observe the unities contributed, for Sidney, to an impression that English drama was in chaos. What he writes appears to be based on actual theatregoing:

> … how all their plays be neither right tragedies nor right comedies, mingling kings and clowns, not because the matter so carrieth it, but thrust in the clown by head and shoulders to play a part in majestical matters, with neither decency nor discretion, so as neither the admiration and commiseration nor the right sportfulness is by their mongrel tragicomedy obtained … I know the ancients have one or two examples of tragicomedies, as Plautus hath *Amphitryo* … having indeed no right comedy in that comical part of our tragedy, we have nothing but scurrility unworthy of any chaste ears, or some extreme show of doltishness. (Sidney 2004: 46–7)

We don't know what plays Sidney may have seen, but Elizabethan drama provides many examples of serious plays being punctured by the appearance of the mischievous Vice figure familiar in medieval morality plays, and of comic asides occurring at otherwise poignant tragic moments. As Janette Dillon says, 'comic matter is alive and well, kicking its way into every possible dramatic shape' (Dillon 2002: 48). Dillon perceives a serious attempt made by such dramatists as George Peele and John Lyly, commencing in 1583–4, to respond to Sidney's call for more tightly and responsibly structured comic drama. In the passage cited above, Sidney allows for the possibility that there could be 'right comedy in that comical part of our tragedy'. This is a gauntlet thrown down to dramatists to devise responsible mixed forms, a challenge that the Italian dramatist Guarini was accepting virtually while Sidney was writing these words in the *Defence*. *Il Pastor Fido* (*The Faithful Shepherd*) had its first performance in 1585 and first saw print in 1590, but it was begun in the early 1580s and was many times revised. An account of the play is necessary to establish some elements foundational to the new form that will be adopted by later English practitioners.

Set in the imaginary pastoral landscape of Arcadia, the action takes place in the shadow of death, in a society polluted at source in ways not entirely dissimilar from that of Oedipus' Thebes. In Arcadian history, the goddess Cinthia/Diana has cursed society with a plague because of Lucrina's sexual treachery towards Amintas. Lucrina is to be sacrificed, but she and Amintas both commit suicide on the altar. An oracle interprets the goddess's subsequent will: that a virgin should be sacrificed annually, and that any woman discovered in sexual dishonour should be executed. Sex and death are thus inextricably woven into the fabric of Arcadian society. This curse can only be lifted when a young couple of immortal descent are married. For this reason, Silvio the son of Montano, descended from Hercules, and Amarilli the daughter of Titiro, descended from Pan, have been espoused. But there is a problem. Silvio is homoerotically obsessed by hunting and is an enemy to love, just as is Adonis in

Shakespeare's later poem *Venus and Adonis* (1593–4). Amarilli thinks of him as a sexually immature boy. She herself is in love with Mirtillo, a poor foreigner recently arrived in Arcadia and working as a shepherd. We needn't recount in detail the plot twists through which Silvio is married off to Dorinda, having discovered love when he has near-fatally wounded her with an arrow; while Amarilli's rival, the wicked Corisca, fails in her attempts to compromise Amarilli's honour and have her killed. When Corisca's plans to set Amarilli up go awry and Mirtillo, rather than Corisca's dupe Coridon, is discovered in a cave with Amarilli, the play's 'faithful shepherd' is prepared to be sacrificed in Amarilli's stead. Late in the final act, he is discovered to be Montano's lost son, long presumed dead but found and raised by Carino. The blind prophet Tirenio is brought onstage to explain how the discovery of Mirtillo's true identity fulfils the oracle's demands and heals Arcadia (see Figure 2).

Figure 2 *Engraving by Giuseppe Daniotto from* Parnaso Italiano *published in Venice in 1788. Action from Guarini's* Il Pastor Fido, *Act* 3, Scene 3, *depicting the characters of Amarilli, Corisca and Mirtillo. Photo by DEA PICTURE LIBRARY/Getty Images.*

Vitally for the development of tragicomedy, *Il Pastor Fido* permits high-born semi-divine characters Silvio and Amarilli to inhabit the same dramatic world as the poverty-stricken foreigner Mirtillo, albeit Mirtillo is a foundling whose true identity is not established until the end. Before the decorum of social rank is restored, Mirtillo establishes an 'outcast' perspective. Here, we quote from the first English translation of the play published in 1602, attributed to John and Charles Dymock:

> I know too well,
> The lowlinesse of my poore humble starre,
> My desteny's to burne! not to delight
> Was *I* brought forth
>
> (1.2)

This outsider perspective allies Mirtillo with the play's 'Satyr', a scarcely human figure who develops a rich misogynistic vein, articulating the critique, familiar in Italianate English drama of the period, that, with women, what you see is not necessarily what you get:

> Their care, their pompe, and all their whole delight,
> Is in the barke of a bepainted face ...
> O what a stinking thing it is, to see them take
> A Pencill vp, and paint their bloudlesse cheeks ...
>
> (1.5)

The mythological dimensions and elements of classical tragedy are permitted to coexist, in *Il Pastor Fido*, with powerfully satirical speeches that have some social purchase. Although much of the play deals in 'dark materials' and the action proceeds against the ever-present threat of imminent death, Guarini takes out an insurance policy, so to speak, against the worst-case scenario coming to pass. Early in the play, Montano recalls, for Titiro's benefit, the flood that took away his son, going on to tell Amarilli's father of a dream he has recently had:

> there rose me thought an aged man:
> His head and beard dropping downe siluer teares,
> Who gently raught to me with both his hands
> A naked childe, saying, behold thy soone,
> Take heed thou killst him not.
>
> (1.4)

From out a plane tree, there issues 'a subtill voyce / Which said, *Arcadia* shal be faire againe'.

Such reassurances cannot be lost on an audience that must, at whatever level of awareness, realize that the play is inoculated against its own worst outcomes. They must be aware that what they are watching is not a tragedy, even if the generic blueprint is unfamiliar to them. The blunders and accidents that they have witnessed Corisca making in her bloodthirsty attempt to have Amarilli taken while committing a sex crime and executed do not altogether suggest that Corisca is in charge of events or that something tragically inevitable, as Aristotle required of tragedy, is taking place. Consequences resulting from her inept villainy *are* avoidable and the audience must have some inkling that they *will* be avoided. Almost subliminally, audiences are presented with the possibility of the restoration of a lost heir, of the damage done to society by some initial act of pollution being cleansed by a future act of self-sacrifice such as the faithful shepherd Mirtillo offers. Unlike, say, Iago in Shakespeare's *Othello*, who, when confronted with his villainy refuses to acknowledge it, the chief villainess in *Il Pastor Fido* is given an opportunity to acknowledge her wrongdoing and repent, as does Corisca here:

> Ah me it is too true, this is the fruite
> Thou from thy store of vanities must reape …
> Who opens now mine eyes? Ah wretch, I see
> My fault most foule that seem'd felicitie.
>
> (5.9)

However much of *Il Pastor Fido* is spent in the shadow of the sacrificial knife, the redemption of society and not its ruin is the play's objective: healing, not horror.

In 1602, Guarini attached to a new edition of *Il Pastor Fido* a defence of his play which had by then become controversial for destroying the clarity of Aristotle's account of the pure dramatic forms of comedy and tragedy – even if that clarity only existed in the interpretations of the commentators. Surprisingly, his *Compendio della Poesia Tragicomica* was not translated into English and there is still no full translation available as far as I am aware, so it is worth summarizing his discussion. Tragicomedy is not composed of two parallel independent stories, insists Guarini. Together, properly combined, they give life to a new form. Low-born characters can be at the centre of events, he argues contrary to Aristotle, and it is important to represent human reality in all its shades. Guarini lists various elements that are components of his tragicomedy, almost providing a recipe for cooking one up: a noble character (not necessarily high-born), richness of action, both true and fantastical storylines, affections held at bay, entertainments such as hunting, danger without death, laughter and pleasure though moderate, and a happy ending.

One of Guarini's main concerns is to find a dramatic form that strengthens the human spirit; tragedy, he is afraid, may simply sap it. He distinguishes the 'instrumental' (*fine instrumentale*) aspects of a drama from its 'architectural' (*fine architettonico*) impulse, by which he seems to mean a play's structure as against its meaning or purpose. The 'instrumental' imitation of tragic and comic events results, he affirms, in an architecture capable of relieving the deep melancholy of the human spirit. Guarini seems uncertain that, in a modern period armed with Christian faith, the Aristotelian values of pity and terror are appropriate. But, he insists, if pleasure is to be injected into a serious action, it needs to be responsible pleasure: not obscenity or vulgar scenes of disrespect. He insists on and defends vigorously the unity of tragicomedy and in particular of *Pastor Fido*. The latter pages of the *Compendio* insist that tragicomedy is an imitation not of things as they *are*, but of things as they *could be*. Guarini distinguishes real truth from 'verisimilitude', which implies probability but is an ideal implementation of the universal. This will be an important argument for John Fletcher when his 1608 tragicomedy *The Faithful Shepherdess* is damned by an unsympathetic public, discussed more fully below. Guarini's main purpose was to defend his blended drama against Aristotelian generic purism, but he also gave thought to the question of how the audience would experience that new mixture. He attended to the technical difficulties of how to manage information in order to maximize surprise and suspense, to avoid 'scemare la maraviglia, e'n consequenza il diletto' (spoiling the marvel and in the consequence, the delight) (Guarini 1914: 282). This is an issue that will arise in later English tragicomedy, when the label can seem to give too much of the game away. Guarini's discussion is high-minded, often abstract and always repetitive, but he never leaves the theatre entirely behind.

Enter Shakespeare

And so enter Shakespeare. We don't know whether Shakespeare ever read *Il Pastor Fido* or Guarini's *Discourse*. In support of the possibility, the Italian language had been opened up through the 1598 publication of John Florio's English–Italian dictionary *A World of Words*; and there has been scholarly speculation that Florio, who shared a patron with Shakespeare (the Earl of Southampton), was a personal friend who may have taught the dramatist some Italian. His wife has even been offered as a candidate for the Dark Lady of the *Sonnets*. Lois Potter's biography suggests that Shakespeare had 'probably worked his way through' the *Compendio* in Italian (Potter 2012: 340). If so, he would have seen theorized a type of drama that blended comedy with tragedy and begun to understand how pity might operate in a Christian society. Recall Guarini's point that, in a fideistic society, the unrelieved nature of Aristotelian terror might not have a legitimate function. If there is a benign deity, and there is an afterlife in which redeemed souls enjoy unbounded felicity, tragedies ending in piles of corpses are not the end of the story.

Shakespeare was entirely familiar with the fictional stories written by the Italian novelists Matteo Bandello and Giraldi Cinthio. He might possibly have known something of the Anglo-European discussion of mixed drama to which, as we remarked, Cinthio contributed. He used Cinthio's story in the *Hecatommithi* (1565) as the principal source for *Othello* and another of the stories for *Measure for Measure*. If Shakespeare did not know the *Compendio*, he nevertheless became deeply involved in the experiment to produce successful happy-ending tragedies. *Much Ado About Nothing*, a play that also has a source in Cinthio, anticipates the more theorized, more purposive tragicomedy *Measure for Measure*, written after Guarini became available in English. There is a strong probability that he had read Sidney's *Defence*, which, as we have seen, taps into the early discussion of mixed drama. Touchstone's punning conversation with the bemused Audrey in *As You Like It* 3.3.13–24 is based on Sidney's argument that poetry is more effective than history because it is not tied to actual facts. Shakespeare followed literary discussion about drama closely enough to play with its ideas, as is demonstrated in *As You Like It* – not itself a tragicomedy, but clearly suffused in, and in dialogue with, the fashionable pastoral of Sidney and Spenser and, through them, at a remove, the Italians.

Towards the end of the century, Shakespeare was experimenting with a controlled form of mixed drama combining tragic and comic elements. *Much Ado About Nothing*, first published in 1600 but written late 1598 or early 1599, already provided an uncomfortable dramatic experience in which the death of the heroine is compassed – appears actually to have occurred – but in which, through the mechanism of penitence and 'resurrection', a happy ending is contrived. The secondary plot couple, for whom there is no source, are Beatrice and Benedick, characterized through their wit-combats that borrow features from John Lyly and his highly stylized, elaborately patterned rhetoric described as 'euphuistic' after Lyly's prose works *Euphues: An Anatomy of Wit* (1578) and *Euphues and His England* (1580). By the end of 3.1, however, this seemingly anti-romantic couple has been tricked and converted, much to the audience's mirth, to the sloppiest kind of mutual adoration. In the main plot, meanwhile, such is the condition of mutual distrust in Shakespeare's Sicily that Hero's father Leonato and lover Claudio prefer to believe in a malicious attempt to frame her as unfaithful, rather than in Hero's obviously sincere denial of it. Her marriage to Claudio is viciously and cruelly aborted, though the Friar has already proposed an escape route, providing the drama with green shoots of hope.

When Beatrice and Benedick next meet, in 4.1, the wit, punning and bawdy innuendo and all traces of euphuism have vanished from their dialogue. Beatrice is actually tongue-tied:

> **Benedick** I do love nothing in the world so well as you. Is not that strange?
>
> **Beatrice** As strange as the thing I know not. It were as possible for me to say I loved nothing in the world so well as you. But believe me not – and yet I lie not. I confess nothing, nor I deny nothing. I am sorry for my cousin. (4.1.267–72)

Benedick's response to this is a send-up of the conventions of courtly love: 'Come, bid me do anything for thee' (287). He expects to be sent off on a preposterous mission to prove his love like a medieval knight-errant – rather like the wild-goose chases he has proposed to Don Pedro in 2.1.241–9 as a way of avoiding Beatrice's company: 'I will fetch you a toothpicker now from the furthest inch of Asia; bring you the length of Prester John's foot; fetch you a hair off the Great Cham's beard.' But in an electrifying *coup de théâtre*, what Beatrice actually says is 'Kill Claudio'. This is the 'tragicomic moment', producing reactions from audiences that range from uncomfortable laughter to sharp intakes of breath.

The dramatic means through which a happy ending for Claudio and Hero is contrived never sit entirely comfortably with audiences. The passively virtuous heroine goes through a kind of death. The patriarchal figures Claudio and Leonato, the former entirely and the latter slightly less compromised by their distrustful refusal to believe in Hero, are required to take her in an act of blind faith. Claudio must marry her veiled, take on trust what he is asked to do: an antidote to his earlier unwarranted suspicion. Even Benedick has had to swallow that medicine, putting his trust in Beatrice's certainty that Hero has been wronged and agreeing to challenge his friend. There have been throughout wise counsellors and guardian figures – Beatrice, the Friar, the Sexton, and in burlesque fashion the Watch – who have been a form of insurance policy against the worst possibilities materializing. Sicilian society can be healed and its weak and fallen members can have a second chance to put things right. Particularly striking in theatrical effects are the final scenes that deliver a resolved ending. Act 5, Scene 3 is set in the churchyard where Leonato's family tomb is located, utilizing night-light provided by tapers, the reading of a funerary epitaph, a scroll and a solemn promise to honour Hero's memory made in song. Against this ritualized background heavy with death, Claudio asserts his willingness this time to fulfil his promise, even if not in terms that would meet with present-day approval: 'I'll hold to my mind were she an Ethiope' (5.4.38). And Hero is quasi-magically restored to life.

Marston

On 5 July 1604, the printers William Aspley and Thomas Thorpe paid their sixpence fee to enter a literary property in the Stationers' Register, the function of which is explained earlier in the Introduction: 'Entred for their Copie vnder the handes of Master Pasfeild and Master Norton warden an

Enterlude called the Malecontent [,] Tragiecomedia.' Likely though it is that the label 'tragiecomedia' was picked up from an authorial manuscript and therefore was John Marston's own designation, he appeared to be in some doubt about what genre it was. The 1604 printed edition is dedicated in Latin to Ben Jonson, where the play is described as 'asperam hanc suam Thaliam' (this harsh comedy of his); again in the preface 'To the Reader', Marston refers to it as a 'satire' and as a 'Comedy'. An Induction written for the play by John Webster stages members of the cast puzzling over it:

> **Sly.** Do you hear, sir, this play is a bitter play?
>
> **Condell.** Why, sir, 'tis neither satire nor moral, but the mean passage of a history. (Marston 1975: 11)

Many clues are planted in the text, however, to suggest that Marston intended *The Malcontent* to be the first play in English that would take on board Guarini's generic experiment in *Il Pastor Fido*.

Although the surface textures of the two plays are not at all alike – *The Malcontent* takes place in the entirely corrupted environment of the Genoese court, whereas *Pastor Fido* is set in the idealized bucolic landscape of Arcadia – Marston's play is peppered with quotations from and allusions to the Italian play. One quotation operates almost like a secret code, identifying the play's genre. The usurped Duke Altofront currently haunts the court of his usurper Pietro disguised as Malevole, a railing, biting satirist constantly commenting on the depraved, septic, filthy aspects of court society. Pietro says of him that 'his highest delight is to procure others vexation' (1.2.21–2), and here he is in typically disagreeable conversation with a nitwitted chamberlain called Bilioso.

> **Mal.** O Hercules!
>
> **Bil.** Hercules? Hercules was the son of Jupiter and Alcmena.

Mal. Your Lordship is a very wittol.

Bil. Wittol?

Mal. Ay, all-wit.

Bil. Amphitryo was a cuckold.

(4.5.95–100)

A 'wittol' was a cuckold – not a compliment; further to bait Bilioso, Malevole turns the word on its head as 'all-wit', a wordplay familiar in this period. Talk of cuckolds seems suddenly to put Amphitryo, cuckolded by the god Jupiter, into Bilioso's cottonwool brain. George Hunter, editor of the Revels Plays edition of *The Malcontent*, throws up his hands in despair when trying to explain this passage: 'Bilioso's worry about the cuckolding of Amphitryon by Jupiter and Alcmena is very strangely woven into this dialogue. Perhaps some lines are misplaced' (125n.) My readers will recall that Plautus' *Amphitruo* was the ancient prototype of the tragicomedy. Reference to it here functions almost as a mason's mark on a building, a sign setting *The Malcontent* in the tragicomic tradition. Marston's play is indebted to *Pastor Fido* in many places, so many as to suggest that he had read the Dymocks' 1602 translation just before he began writing it. One example might serve. Mendoza is the arch-villain, lover of Pietro's wife Aurelia, who spurns him in Act 1 because she has taken on another lover, Ferneze. This provokes a misogynistic diatribe from Mendoza: women are 'rash in asking, desperate in working, impatient in suffering, extreme in desiring, slaves unto appetite, mistresses in dissembling, only constant in unconstancy, only perfect in counterfeiting' (1.6.88–91), a passage directly based on the Satyr's similar outburst in *Pastor Fido* 1.5.

Act 4, Scene 5 is an excellent example of a scene that audiences would recognize as tragicomic once they became more familiar with the form. Malevole and Pietro, the latter disguised as a hermit, have just discovered that Mendoza has put them up to murdering one another. They meet with Aurelia who believes her Duke Pietro to be dead. Aurelia is overcome with shame and remorse. Pietro suggests that she visit his cell, where the working through of her penitence will be assisted by its 'rheumy vault' and 'rocky barrenness'. Anguished and contrite, Aurelia is drawn by her disguised husband into a full confession of her adultery with Mendoza and her unpardonable ingratitude towards Pietro. As she exits, Malevole 'comforts' Pietro with a catalogue of mythical heroes who were all *cornutos* (cuckolds), the texture here at considerable variance from Aurelia's exalted self-blame just witnessed:

> **Mal.** Hercules, whose back bore up heaven, and got forty wenches with child in one night –
>
> **Pietro.** Nay, 'twas fifty.
>
> **Mal.** Faith, forty's enow, a' conscience – yet was a *cornuto*. (4.5.58–61)

Oddly comical that Pietro should insist on getting the number of Hercules' bastards correct at a time like this, when he has just heard his wife's confession. Malevole continues to 'be his affliction', when the mincing, flattering courtier Bilioso enters and has the exchange noted above. Bilioso's exit is followed by a rhetorical set-piece in which Malevole advises Pietro towards *contemptus mundi*: renounce this world, 'the very muck-hill on which the sublunary orbs cast their excrements' and in which 'Man is the slime of this dung-pit'. (Around the same date, 1603–4, Shakespeare was composing a similar speech in a parallel dramatic situation in *Measure for Measure* 3.1.5ff., when Duke Vincentio, disguised as a friar, tries to persuade the condemned Claudio to renounce life in a famous speech commencing 'Be absolute for death'.)

This wrings from Pietro a confession of his own guilt as usurper and an avowal of his determination to do what he can to set things right. The result is a *coup de théâtre*:

O, I am changed; for here, 'fore the dread power,
In true contrition I do dedicate
My breath to solitary holiness,
My lips to prayer; and my breast's care shall be,
Restoring Altofront to regency.
Mal. Thy vows are heard, and we accept thy faith.
Undisguiseth himself.
(4.5.127–32)

Malevole the biting satirist is revealed to be none other than Duke Altofronto, whose dukedom Pietro has usurped. The elements here of repentance, with a determination to do right, followed by a stage effect that strikes the beholders with amazement and wonder, enabling the possibility of grace and forgiveness, are already to be found in the prototypical tragicomedy *Much Ado About Nothing* that Shakespeare had already written and in those that he would go on to write, commencing with *Measure for Measure* in 1603–4.

Disguise

The period 1602–4, that witnessed the influence of Guarini through the Dymock translation of *Il Pastor Fido* and Guarini's defence of it, also saw the return of a theatrical element that would become significant in the history of tragicomedy: disguise. King James's account of kingship, *Basilikon Doron* (1599), was reissued in 1603 to coincide with his succession. Emphasizing that kings should be more observers than active participants, that they should be retired rather than prominent, James put dramatists in mind of George Whetstone's influential *A Mirour for Magestrates of Cyties* (1584). This prose treatise was an account of the Emperor Severus' wholesale reform of Rome following the horrors and excesses of his predecessor Heliogabalus. Not content with reform, Severus demands that the Senate institute a thoroughgoing surveillance regime:

> ye better to search the core of vice & iniquitie hid in the intrailes of *Rome*. These good Maiestrats vsed this pollicie, in disguysed habits they entred ye Tauerns, common tables, victuling houses, stewes & brothel-harbors, without controlement, they viewed ye behauiors of the people, that thei might the better vnderstand the ful of their abuses. (Whetstone 1584: 3)

Whetstone's premise of a society fallen into lewdness, luxury and vice, cured by a reforming potentate operating through undercover agents, appeared to chime with King James's ideas on governance and is picked up in Thomas Middleton's play *The Phoenix*, probably written in 1603. Here, the Duke of Ferrara's son Phoenix goes into disguise, accompanied by his trusted servant Fidelio, their intention being to 'set in frame / A kingdom all in pieces'. They witness adultery, incest, theft, treason, bribery, attempted murder and in a vivid scene a sea-captain's attempt to sell his wife, who also happens to be Fidelio's mother. *The Phoenix* is classified as a tragicomedy in the authoritative collection of Middleton's *Works* (2007), though one might think of it as not a fully formed example. Its dramatic structure is a series of outrages witnessed by Prince Phoenix whose interventions set society to rights. Set-piece speeches on the law and matrimony establish an uncomplicated perspective on what is morally necessary for society to function well and Phoenix is an unequivocal force for good.

Marston's *The Malcontent* presents Altofront in disguise throughout much of the play. In 1.4, he explains to Celso why he has taken on the disguised persona of Malevole, the spiteful, railing satirist. Until now, he has been too naïve, lacking 'those old instruments of state, / Dissemblance and Suspect' (1.4.9–10). He was not enough of a Machiavel, it appears, to prevent his banishment by Pietro and conspirators allied with Florence. (Shakespeare's Duke in *Measure for Measure* [1604] and later his Prospero in *The Tempest* [1611] provide a similar explanation of usurpation.) His disguise offers him 'Free speech', 'a tongue / As fetterless as is an emperor's' (1.3.162, 164–5). Although more complex than Middleton's use of the disguised Duke in *The Phoenix*, Marston's deployment is still relatively straightforward. As G. K. Hunter expresses it, 'the tragicomic structure ensures that Malevole and Altofront, the libertine and the moralist, are not simply alternating responses ... but simultaneous aspects of a unified view of the world' (Marston 1975: lxviii). As Malevole, Altofront can criticize the venal acquisitiveness of a fallen court, and as Altofront, he can provide the moral conscience capable of renewing the social contract.

Where there is a disguised Duke – in *The Malcontent* there are two, when Pietro dons 'a hermit's gown and beard' in 3.5 – the audience apprehends that all is not as it seems, that identities are temporary and that unexpected results may transpire. A play whose texture is impenetrably dark and coruscatingly satirical nevertheless finds space for a Frenchified female procurer Maquerelle, and a sexual clown, Passarello, the latter possibly a later addition. The audience is surprised early on when Mendoza's plan to have his rival Ferneze caught in the act and murdered in Aurelia's chamber does *not* result in Ferneze's death. In other plays of the period, certain death would have resulted. Seemingly dead, Ferneze 'stirs' at the end of Act 2 and is helped offstage by Malevole in a kind of resurrection. Such 'resurrections' were introduced by Shakespeare in *Much Ado*, as we have seen, and would continue to be important in Shakespearean tragicomedy.

Re-enter Shakespeare: *Measure for Measure*

Shakespeare and Marston appear to have worked in competition or in friendly collusion since around 1601. There are parallels between *Hamlet* and Marston's *Antonio's Revenge* sufficiently close to suggest that the two dramatists were aware of each other's work even if access to a common source cannot be definitively ruled out as an explanation.

No scholar who has worked on the subject believes that the parallels are coincidental. Professionally self-aware writers working in such close proximity are likely to have kept abreast of each other's projects. Neither *The Malcontent* nor *Measure for Measure* can be dated with certainty but the first known performance of *Measure for Measure* was at Whitehall on 26 December 1604 – the records of the Revels Office show a performance of 'A Play called Mesur for Mesur' by 'Shaxberd' – suggesting that Marston's play might have predated it. Both plays present a duke who has fallen down on the job, resulting in a disintegrating society. Both dukes perceive a remedy in assuming a disguise. There are verbal echoes between the two plays suggestive of influence (Shakespeare 1991: 18n.1). Both plays have somewhere in mind the accession of a new king, James VI and I, who, as we have noted, expressed strong views on kingship in a recently republished treatise, *Basilikon Doron* (1603), offering advice on rulership to his son Prince Henry. Indeed, the suggestion is made that Henry might actually assume a disguise to see further into his subjects' actions and opinions: 'And therefore delite to haunt your Session, and spie carefully their proceedings' (45).

Discussion of *Measure for Measure* is complicated because the only available text, that published in the 1623 First Folio, is likely to have been doctored by Thomas Middleton in 1621. John Jowett's 'genetic' text of the play argues that the setting, Vienna, was an alteration by Middleton relevant to the political context in the 1620s. Shakespeare's original setting may have been Ferrara – the setting for Middleton's *Phoenix* and incidentally the town where Guarini held a professorial position. Jowett indicates several passages that may be adaptations by Middleton, the cumulative effect of which is to intensify the satirical dimension. In 1603–4, Marston and Shakespeare were both seeing the potential of tragicomedy not so much in terms of *pastoral*, the form pioneered by Guarini, as in urban satire.

We now have the benefit of the recently published Arden Third Series edition of *Measure for Measure*. The Arden editors do not accept the designation 'tragicomedy':

> This play has very little of the atmosphere that evidently made that genre so popular just a few years later: exotic locations, survival of shipwrecks, glimpses of the supernatural, children and their parents separated and then reunited, with the native nobility of royal blood shining through adversity and rusticity. (Shakespeare 2020: 3)

They speak of the play as signalling 'resistance to the genres of pastoral and tragicomic romance by subjugating their key elements' (4). To that I would respond that *theatrical* tragicomic romance is not yet a genre at all. It is still on the anvil. Robert Watson is right that Shakespeare's later, more developed tragicomedy borrows more memes from romance.[1] What is already developed in *Measure*, however, is what I have called in the Introduction the metaphysics of the 'second chance', one of the chief *raisons d'être* of an intermediate genre. This play deploys the word 'grace' twenty-one times and the word 'mercy' on sixteen occasions, more frequently than any other Shakespeare play. Watson acknowledges the 'tragicomic trinity' of mercy, grace and penitence when he speaks of the Duke's 'determination to give even such persevering reprobates as Lucio and Barnardine another chance at repentance' (33). His own discussion of the play's ending contains material that might tell against his rejection of tragicomedy. He points to the pastoral strain introduced into the play by the sequestered Mariana; and to *coups de théâtre* through which several characters emerge from disguise amidst an ethos of forgiveness. And the Duke's final speech that gives onto a notoriously indeterminate ending is very significant here. Into it, he slips what appears to be a marriage proposal to Isabella:

> Dear Isabel,
> I have a motion much imports your good,
> Whereto if you'll a willing ear incline,
> What's mine is yours, and what is yours is mine.
> (5.1.534–7)

Frequently in modern productions, the void space created by the absence of a recorded response from Isabella is written into by directors, who make clear that such a proposal is coercive and unwelcome. Sometimes she even slaps his face. Since that utterly destroys the possibility of an entirely happy ending, it results in a perception that the play cannot be a tragicomedy. But Watson himself argues that this does not feel like a Shakespearean ending; indeed, he accepts that, like the earlier proposal at 5.1.492–3, it might have been one of Middleton's revisionist interventions (122–3).

Critics and audiences have discovered two plays in *Measure for Measure*: the first centring on the 'realistic', debating scenes between Isabella and Angelo, 2.2 and 2.4, where the question of the nature of justice is discussed. Is the law a system of prescriptions to be applied without recourse to context and interpretation? Or can it be applied humanely? This partly involves a clash between Old and New Testament ideas of law, the play's title cueing us into those issues through its allusion to Matthew 7.1–2 and to the Sermon on the Mount. In 2.2 and 2.4, the question answers itself because, as the issues are debated between Angelo and Isabella, the former becomes irresistibly erotically attracted to the movements of Isabella's mind and to the passion with which she expresses herself. Angelo becomes the living proof of the falsehood involved in his own impersonal and abstract interpretation of law and religion. Commencing in 3.1, a second play seems to veer away from compelling individual psychology and into the mechanics of an overcomplicated plot. But the relationship between the 'realistic' and the 'romantic' elements of the play are intelligible in terms of Guarini's mixed-mode tragicomedy outlined in his *Compendio* (Figure 3).

Despite the widespread reaction that the second half of the play entirely alters in atmosphere, Shakespeare's tragicomic prototype does not altogether present a serious quasi-tragic first half, followed by a comic plot-dominated second half, whether we place the 'hinge' at the beginning of 3.1 or of 4.1. (Act and scene divisions were in any case not a feature of plays pre-1609 and were probably another of Middleton's editorial changes to this text.) The condemnation of Claudio is framed by a scene, 1.2, in which Pompey, Mistress Overdone and Lucio

Figure 3 *Rory Kinnear as Angelo and Anna Maxwell Martin as Isabella in* Measure for Measure, *directed by Michael Attenborough at the Almeida Theatre, London, 2010. Photo by robbie jack/Corbis via Getty Images.*

are already constructing their carnal vision of a society where prostitution, sexually transmitted diseases and pregnancy out of wedlock are, if not normat*ive*, then certainly the norm. Angelo's dark tyranny and sexual malfeasance struggles to get itself taken seriously in a society incompetently policed by Elbow, prompting Escalus' exclamation 'Which is the wiser here, Justice or Iniquity?' (2.1.165). Audience concentration on Isabella's plea before Angelo in 2.2 is distracted throughout by Lucio's attempt to direct it as a play within a play: 'You are too cold … Aye, touch him, there's the vein … Oh, to him, to him, wench, he will relent.' The focus is as much on him as it is on Isabella's searching out of the weak mortality behind Angelo's absolutist pose. Similar stagecraft will recur in *The Winter's Tale*, where again serious scenes will be hijacked for an entirely different mood. Even the powerful brother–sister encounter in 3.1, where Claudio's fear of death dissolves his initial strength of will, is filtered by the fact that the disguised

Duke and apparently also the Provost are voyeurs throughout. We do not experience a duologue in the same way as we experience an observed duologue. While Isabella stigmatizes her brother's fear of death as cowardice and 'a kind of incest', her own fetishizing of chastity can horrify an audience as much. Before the end of the scene, a mechanism has been proposed – the Mariana bed-trick – by means of which Isabella, Claudio and Mariana might find succour.

The remainder of the play does not merely rig up a set of strings and pulleys through which society is to be healed. It also shows that the Duke, whatever he may think, is not in control of the process and perhaps does not have the moral stature ever to be so. Ambiguous characters such as the Duke and Angelo are echoed in the supporting roles: witness Lucio, whose refusal to assist the imprisoned Pompey is breathtakingly unkind. His 'the world must be peopled' attitude has its appeal and when he complains against Angelo that 'this ungenitured agent will unpeople the province with continency' (3.1.431–3), he allies himself sympathetically with the force of 'natural' carnality. Within a few lines, however, it turns out that Mistress Overdone is committed to prison for brothel-keeping on Lucio's information and that he, like Angelo, has broken a marriage vow! Act 3 ends with an incantatory rhyming soliloquy delivered by the Duke that has a choric function as do the later figures of Time in *The Winter's Tale* and of Gower in *Pericles*. It prefigures a change of location and tone in 4.1, partially explained by material introduced by Middleton at a later stage. Yet still, however clearly the Duke seems to understand his moral function as expressed in the choric speech, he will go on in malfeasance and to commit blunders. In 4.2.79, he tells the Provost of Angelo's 'holy abstinence' knowing that to be false. By 4.3, he seems literally to have lost the plot. The action that presents Barnardine's refusal to be hanged borders on farce, exacerbated by the fortuitous death of Ragozine, 'A man of Claudio's years, his beard and head, / Just of his colour' (4.3.70–1). When the Duke comments 'Oh, 'tis an accident that heaven provides' (75), the point is underlined that it is not the Duke, but 'heaven', the power of Providence, that is going to sort this mess out. His justification for what audiences experience as his most unpardonable lie – telling Isabella that her brother has been executed – is that it will 'make her heavenly comforts of despair / When it is least expected' (108–9). She is then enjoined to 'give [her] cause to heaven' (122).

A playwright's justification for the spun-out ending would be that it maximizes the effect of surprise and reversal of fortune. Tragicomic form, as Shakespeare is defining it, however, requires the elaborate working-out of providential justice: 'a physic / That's bitter to sweet end' as Isabella puts the point at 4.6.7–8. There is a power beyond the human that deploys mercy and grace to put right what even the most socially powerful of human beings cannot rectify alone. Amidst the revelations of Act 5, Lucio's purpose is to be a distraction similar to his earlier functioning. Whatever the gravitas of Angelo's depravity being unmasked, however far he has strayed from 'weigh[ing] thy brother by himself' (5.1.111), Lucio's mosquito-like presence remains to undermine the solemnity in tragicomic mode; his backbiting is the final enormity resolved by the Duke. The play ends with the actual staging of mercy and charity. The Christian dispensing of New Testament modes of justice must be seen to be done, as Claudio 'resurrects' in similar fashion to Hero, returning from the dead. Angelo gets a second bite at life's cherry because he is a penitent.

All's Well That Ends Well

Attempts to trace the development of Shakespeare's tragicomic form are bedevilled, as we have seen, by difficulties of chronology and authorship. *All's Well That Ends Well* presents similar problems to those that occur in *Measure for Measure*. The latest thinking is that it too, in the version we read derived from the 1623 First Folio, reveals the adapting hand of Thomas Middleton. The dating range for *All's Well* is particularly broad but a consensus may be emerging that it was written after *Measure for Measure* in early 1605, and adapted by Middleton sometime between 1616 and 1622, most likely in 1621. In this case, the adaptation makes less difference to an audience's appreciation of the play's mode, though if the coarse conversation about virginity that takes place between Paroles and Helen at 1.1.110–63 (Shakespeare 2019) is by Middleton, it clearly makes some. Audiences are frequently unhappy with this exchange, one that establishes a character for Helen that is not wholly compatible with her subsequent deportment in the play. Her sexuality is unusually frank, certainly – and the language of curing the King is also a language of *seducing* him – but this exchange comes close to cynical bawdry.

If indeed *All's Well* is later than *Measure*, it can be seen as another exercise in tragicomic form, a further attempt to stabilize the 'formula' and render it repeatable – but one that does not quite work. It is a tragicomedy *manqué*. The first two acts are dominated by romance motifs – Helen's quasi-magical curative powers and the Cinderella-style marriage to her social superior Bertram as the reward for those take the play in a fairy-tale direction. But Bertram's abandonment of his newly wedded wife turns it towards prodigality and pilgrimage. As does *Measure*, successful plot-resolution depends on the bed-trick, a device that does not appear to have been outside the contemporary comfort zone, however awkwardly it sits with ours today. There are many elements that we are identifying as constitutive of the tragicomic. There are, in *All's Well*, safeguards against worst-case scenarios that we have suggested are almost subliminally transmitted to audiences: the Countess of Rousillon can be regarded as a 'protector' figure, while Paroles and Lavatch both provide the kinds of comic distraction for which Lucio is responsible in *Measure*, continuing even at times of solemnity and danger in the play and unsettling the tone.

The play's final scene has many elements in common with the ending of *Measure for Measure* – elements that will define tragicomedy in Shakespeare's handling of it. Once again, the justice meted out to the wronged women Helen and Diana is elaborately worked out, prolonged by obstacles and wrong turnings. Again, this is justice being *seen* to be done. Material evidence in the shape of Helen's ring, now mysteriously (to Bertram) in Diana's hands, is produced. Paroles functions as does Lucio in *Measure*, providing equivocal testimony that introduces an incongruously comical note to the proceedings. Again, quasi-resurrection is part of the healing process: Helen's death is reported but, when she returns, she returns teeming with new life: 'one that's dead is quick' (5.3.301). Death, resurrection, rebirth: the repeated terms 'grace' and 'sanctity', two words that echo throughout the play, as do 'grace' and 'mercy' in *Measure* – all this imparts some sense of a ritual cleansing of society. That is heightened by metrical devices already encountered in *Measure for Measure*. As Act 3 closes, the Duke delivers an incantatory, sententious speech in tetrameter rhyming couplets, reflecting on his own moral duty:

> He who the sword of heaven will bear
> Should be as holy, as severe:
> Pattern in himself to know,
> Grace to stand, and virtue go.
>
> (3.2.223–6)

Such metrical sound effects are even more a feature of *All's Well*, which embeds sonnets, riddles and incantations.

So why is this a tragicomedy *manqué*? Even more markedly than *Measure for Measure*, which falls short of satisfactory closure, *All's Well* seems to defy it – to the extent, indeed, that the play's title can be interpreted as an irony. Bertram's conditional acceptance of Helen is not even addressed directly to her but is spoken through the King: 'If she, my liege, can make me know this clearly, / I'll love her dearly, ever, ever dearly' (5.3.313–14). What is the import of the faintly mocking rhyming couplet here? 'If' has been shown to govern the entire play, putting its action in the conditional mood, culminating in Bertram's acceptance of Helen only upon conditions. Bertram does not exhibit anything like the penitence of Angelo, though neither is he so criminal; and overall, the materials of *All's Well* are not as dark as those of *Measure*. Nevertheless, the latter play probably provides a more satisfactory sense of lessons learned and disasters avoided, of the obstacles to marriage having been removed and of Isabella's possible salvation from a misguided life in a nunnery. Angelo earns his second chance through penitence and subsequent grace. Bertram seems neither to earn it nor to want it. *All's Well*, in short, is not a 'feelgood' play. Shakespeare's later tragicomedies will strive harder to achieve the feelgood factor.

1605–10: Tragicomedy's Decisive Years

Events decisive for the development and rootedness of tragicomedy occurred in this vital five-year period: publication in Madrid in 1605 of that monument of prose fiction, Miguel de Cervantes's *Don Quixote*; periods of theatre closure coinciding with a hiatus in Shakespeare's career that resulted in his resuming a much earlier practice of collaborative writing – with Thomas Middleton, George Wilkins and, most vitally for our topic, John Fletcher; distinctive changes in Shakespeare's dramatic verse style; the acquisition of an indoor playing venue, the Blackfriars, by Shakespeare's troupe the King's Men; and yet another competitive/collaborative episode of playwriting that puts Beaumont and Fletcher's play *Philaster, or Love Lies a-Bleeding* in dialogue with Shakespeare's *Cymbeline*. Let us consider each of them in turn.

After King James's coronation, English culture took a decisively Hispanophile turn. Diplomatic relations were reopened with Spain in 1604 after nearly half a century of continuous rivalry and warfare. When James VI of Scotland ascended the English throne in 1603, a speedy end to

Elizabeth's Spanish wars was a strong expectation placed upon him, duly delivered by the Treaty of London of 1604, ratified in Valladolid in June 1605. Shakespeare's acting company, now called the King's Men and promoted to the status of Grooms of the Chamber, were in attendance on the Constable of Castile's delegation in London in August 1604, displaying their scarlet cloaks and doublets. Although only Phillips and Heminge are specifically named in the King's Treasurer's accounts as being paid for this service, Shakespeare must have been amongst the 'ten of their fellows' who were also remunerated. It is not clear that any plays were performed, but it is difficult to see what else would be done by actors to entertain Spanish grandees, other than taking part in processions. The Revels Accounts for 1604/5 show the King's Men being paid for *Merry Wives*, *Measure for Measure*, *Comedy of Errors* and *Love's Labours Lost*, all by 'Shaxberd', during the Christmas season following (Duncan-Jones 2001: 170–2).

Just as the diplomatic mission to Spain to ratify the Treaty of London was setting out in May 1605, the Madrid publisher Juan de la Cuesta was publishing *El Ingenioso Hidalgo Don Quixote de la Mancha, compuesto por Miguel de Cervantes Saavedra.* There is no evidence to suggest that Shakespeare was amongst the retinue of 506 persons brought by the Earl of Nottingham to Valladolid. What is clear, however, is that, on the return of the diplomatic missionaries, a wave of Cervantine enthusiasm commenced. The Bodleian Library annexed a first edition copy of *Don Quixote* immediately upon publication. That acquisition was funded from a benefaction of £100 donated by the Earl of Southampton, who had been Shakespeare's patron some years earlier (Randall and Boswell 2009: 1–3). The year 1607 defines a first 'Cervantine moment' in English theatrical culture. Around 1606–7, arguably the most significant homage to Cervantes in the entire history of his reception had commenced. Thomas Shelton, an Irish Roman Catholic who had spent much of his life in exile in Spain and the Spanish Netherlands, had begun to translate the first part of *Don Quixote* into English. That translation, published in 1612, remains the bedrock of subsequent English

Quixotes. Its pre-publication circulation is evidenced by the fact that several plays published in 1607 refer to *Don Quixote*: Beaumont's *Knight of the Burning Pestle*, George Wilkins's *The Miseries of Enforced Marriage* and Thomas Middleton's *Your Five Gallants*.

During the same period, a new dramatic career was being launched that would prove essential to the popularization of tragicomedy, that of John Fletcher. Well-born son of the Bishop of London, Fletcher belonged to a family that had lost royal favour by the final years of Elizabeth's reign. Perhaps that loss was behind his decision to pursue a playwriting vocation. His début play, a collaboration with Francis Beaumont entitled *The Woman Hater*, was performed in 1606. Though politically Fletcher was suspicious of Spanish imperial power, he was culturally Hispanophile. Through Francis Beaumont, who was a cousin of Henry Hastings, fifth Earl of Huntingdon, Fletcher gained the patronage of a kinship group – Hastings and the Sidneys – who had long been interested in Spanish romance and culture more broadly (Samson 2009: 23–33). His services and those of Beaumont appear to have been acquired early on by the King's Men; indeed, there is some merit in the argument that Fletcher was part of that company's 'succession planning', a playwright groomed to take over when Shakespeare's career finally came to an end. Records show that in 1611–12, Shakespeare and Fletcher collaborated on a play that has not survived, probably entitled *The History of Cardenio*, based on the Cardenio story told intermittently across a sizeable tranche of *Don Quixote* (Hammond 2010). It seems likely that Fletcher was the moving force in this Cervantic adaptation.

What was Shakespeare doing as Fletcher's career was getting off the mark? After the completion of the major tragedies *King Lear* and *Macbeth*, there was a hiatus. Many Shakespearean scholars agree that when he returned to writing, in 1608 or 1609, his style had changed considerably. Bart Van Es's *Shakespeare in Company* considers anew the question of hiatus and of Shakespeare's 'late style', the widely attested observation that post-1608 Shakespearean drama is very different from much that preceded it (Van Es 2013). His account, in brief, is that, after 1608, Shakespeare's proximity to the acting troupe for whom he wrote roles diminished and he looked elsewhere for artistic inspiration – importantly, to the shaping influence of John Fletcher. Many critics have observed in plays such as *Cymbeline* and *The Winter's Tale* a dissociation between the characters and the language they speak: as Russ McDonald puts it, 'about 1607 or so, Shakespeare begins to weaken the link between speech and speaker' (McDonald 2006: 33–4). Van Es may have found a material cause for this. He identifies 'substantial passages in which Shakespeare strives for effects that another playwright [Fletcher] had made his own' (Van Es 2013: 265) and there follows an analysis of what *The Faithful Shepherdess* and *Philaster* have that Shakespeare appears to want. (Synergies between *Philaster* and *Cymbeline* have long been observed but there has been a reluctance to attribute the direction of influence as being *from* Beaumont and Fletcher *to* Shakespeare.) As for what Fletcher wanted, it was in the work of Cervantes that he discovered 'an individual who is trapped ... into understanding the world through literary conventions ... Ultimately, what the connection with [Cervantes and] Fletcher amounts to is the embrace of conscious literary artifice' (265, 275). Amongst the several explanations that have been given for Shakespeare's turn towards a self-consciously ironic form of romance in his late career, the discovery of Cervantes may be the single most important consideration.

The ellipsis, contortion, syntactic convolution, dependence on parenthesis and other features that comprise Shakespeare's post-1608 style have often been noted. In recent years, linguistic analysts have examined stylistic features that are even further below the radar, so that they cannot be within the conscious manipulation of the author. The widely held explanation of the hiatus in Shakespeare's career has been that the post-1608 plays were pitched at an indoor audience after the procurement of the Blackfriars. That has come to be regarded as only a partial explanation, however, because plays presented at the Blackfriars continued to be performed at the Globe. The political case that the King's Men's greater involvement in James's court is reflected in the plays' inclusion of music, masque and spectacle does not offer a full explanation. Another possibility lies in the fact that the theatres were closed by plague from mid-1608 to early 1610, a period during which many changes of King's company policy might have occurred; and one that did was, in Andrew Gurr's phrase, 'the rise of the Fletcherian repertory' (Gurr 2004: 148). Their direct collaboration commenced with the lost *Cardenio*, but prior to that, Fletcher's investment in tragicomedy was having an effect on Shakespeare.

Put briefly, Cervantes made two major contributions to dramatic storytelling, apparent in the post-1608 solo and collaborative plays of Beaumont, Fletcher and Shakespeare. The 'metatextuality' of *Don Quixote*, its simultaneous narrative progression and citation of the chivalric and epic/romance sources being sent up by the developing story, heightens an awareness of the textual nature of all fiction. Books, in short, are made of other books. The metatextual aspect of Shakespeare's late plays, the respects in which they include references to earlier writers and function as a commentary on *reading*, has been well analysed by Valerie Wayne, one of the major scholars arguing that familiarity with Cervantes is an important factor in creating their referential complexion (Wayne 2012: 217–38). Self-awareness, metatextuality, is one aspect of the Cervantine legacy. The other is tragicomedy itself. Looking at the conclusion of the Cardenio story in *Don Quixote* which Shakespeare and Fletcher made into a play provides a clear idea of what it had to offer Shakespeare and Fletcher in generic terms. Don Fernando advises Cardenio to ponder 'how it was not by chance, but rather by the particular providence and disposition of the heavens, that they had al met together so unexpectedly' (Shelton 1612: 4.9.407). This insistence on providential guidance, and on the outbreak of weeping that accompanies the happy ending, such that 'it seemed, that some grievous and heavy misfortune had betided them all' (409), provides the clue that, in Cervantes' treatment, the Cardenio story is a romantic tragicomedy. Although the dramatic potential of *Don Quixote*, its performability, has been noted, it has not been widely read as tragicomedy. It is only now beginning to be given this kind of consideration. In Spanish reception of Cervantes, the comparison with Shakespeare was not made prior to the nineteenth century, and then only in terms of comic characterization. *Don Quixote* would become an object of contestation between those who considered the Don life-affirmingly comic and those Romantic readers who considered him ineluctably tragic. But there is a middle way. Verna Foster defines 'tragicomedy' straightforwardly, even if not unproblematically, as follows:

> A tragicomedy is a play in which the tragic and the comic both exist but are formally and emotionally dependent on one another, each modifying and determining the nature of the other so as to produce a mixed, tragicomic response in the audience. (Foster 2004: 11)

James Fenton's stage adaptation of *Don Quixote* premiered at the Royal Shakespeare Company (RSC) in February 2016 was striving after just such mixed responses. Act 1 ends with the stage direction '*Don Quixote is brought in in a cage*', an ambivalent visual image encapsulating the Don's aspiration and limitation simultaneously (Fenton 2016: 48).

The tragicomic arc of the *Quixote* is much more apparent once the second part is published in 1615, though it was not available to Shakespeare and Fletcher in the longer form. Many of its key moments are simultaneously pathetically sad and ridiculously comic. They produce a mixed way of regarding human beings as at once divinely inspired and inherently ludicrous, because the 'hero' is an obsessive madman whose desire is to be nobler, grander, better than the ordinary, often base, creatures who populate his world. As the story progresses, the power relationship between the Don and Sancho gradually reverses, Sancho's greed and upward mobility emancipating him from the feudal relationship with his erstwhile master. To focus on a delusional figure as a protagonist is inevitably to produce a reading experience that is simultaneously laughable and painful, to provide the painfully mixed narrative progression that theatrical tragicomedy at its best also affords.

The Faithful Shepherdess

The Faithful Shepherdess was John Fletcher's first solo play, performed probably in 1608 or 1609 (Figure 4a). The very defensive edition of it published in 1610 reeks of injured pride. Commendatory verses by Ben Jonson included in the 1629 edition entitled 'To the Worthy Author, Master John Fletcher' shed some light on why Fletcher was hurt:

> The wise, and many-headed *Bench*, that sits
> Upon the Life, and Death of *Playes*, and *Wits*,
> ... had, before
> They saw it halfe, damd thy whole play, and more,
> Their motives were, since it had not to do
> With vices, which they look'd for, and came to. (Beaumont and Fletcher 1976: vol. 3, 492, ll. 1–2, 7–10)

Figure 4a *Stage set for a production of John Fletcher's* The Faithful Shepherdess *painted by Norman Wilkinson, 1927. Photo by The Print Collector/Alamy Stock Photo.*

THE
FAITHFVLL
Shepheardeſse.

By IOHN FLETCHER.

Printed at London for *R. Bonian* and *H. Walley*, and are to be ſold at the ſpred Eagle ouer againſt the great North dore of S. Paules.

Figure 4b *Title page of the first edition of John Fletcher's* The Faithfull Shepheardesse *(1608/9). Photo by Culture Club/Getty Images.*

Jonson goes on to predict that Fletcher's 'murdered poem' 'shall rise / A glorified work to time, when fire, / Or moths, shall eat what all these fools admire'. Jonson's elitist critique of those who set themselves up as literary judges, 'the wise and many-headed bench', was developed over decades in response to harsh criticism of some of his own plays. He predicts that *The Faithful Shepherdess* will stand the test of time, which it has, though more as an important milestone in theatre history than as a performable play. Its failure was fortunate in one respect: Fletcher was goaded into writing a preface to the reader where he makes the single most important statement about the nature of tragicomedy recorded in the early modern period. He elaborates on Jonson's enigmatic observation that the play failed because it 'had not to do / With vices':

> It is a pastorall Tragie-comedie, which the people seeing when it was plaid, hauing euer had a singuler guift in defining, concluded to be a play of country hired Shepheards, in gray cloakes, with curtaild dogs in strings, sometimes laughing together, and sometimes killing one another: And missing whitsun ales, creame, wa[ssail] & morris-dances, began to be angry. (Beaumont and Fletcher 1976: vol. 3, 497, ll. 3–8)

Fletcher's status-defined perspective is that the shepherds in his play are not *actual* shepherds, nor do they behave in such a manner as might be represented in knockabout plays or farces staged, for instance, in a fairground. They are 'the owners of flockes, and not hyerlings'. And then he produces the passage to be lit up in neon. I have already cited this in the Introduction, but it bears repeating:

> A tragie-comedie is not so called in respect of mirth and killing, but in respect it wants deaths, which is inough to make it no tragedie, yet brings some neere it, which is inough to make it no comedie: which must be a representation of familiar people, with such kinde of trouble as no life be questiond, so that a God is as lawfull in this as in a tragedie,

and meane people as in a comedie. (Beaumont and Fletcher 1976: vol. 3, 497, ll. 20–8)

The preface ends with a wonderfully supercilious gesture of irritation: 'thus much I hope will serue to iustifie my Poem, and make you vnderstand it, to teach you more for nothing, I do not know that I am in conscience bound.'

Readers of this book will be aware that Fletcher's statement on tragicomedy is Guarini in a nutshell – but the play itself is more a witty comment on Guarini than a version of him. Fletcher takes over the Italian mythological framework, giving us a Priest of Pan, a God of the River and a Satyr as characters. Fletcher's Satyr, though, is a good guy without a wicked bone in his body – a more benign version of Shakespeare's Puck. Out of this ancient pastoral form, Fletcher tries to produce a native strain, 'Englishing' the countryside with fairies and wood nymphs, offering a botany of native herbs and simples with which the saintly Clorin heals the sick and injured: clote, horehound, rhamnus, wormwood, sage, marigold, tormentil, narcissus, lysimachus (willow-herb), darnel, celandine, calamint ... readers could learn from it to be their own herbalists! Character names are a blend of Theocritus (Daphnis) and Spenser (Perigot, Thenot). Atmospherically, some scenes are reminiscent of Spenser's *The Shepheard's Calendar*, while the situations of lovers lost in a wood, making repeated identity mistakes as the result of magic, is *Midsummer Night's Dream* without the comedy. Fletcher's villain is the Sullen Shepherd, his villainous nature demonstrated by the fact that he isn't very good at his job:

> ... whose nye starved flockes
> Are alwaies scabby, and infect all sheepe
> They feed withal, whose lambes are ever last [lost],
> And dye before their weaning, and whose dog,
> Lookes, like his maister, leane, and full of scurffe,
> Not caring for the pipe or whistle. (Beaumont and Fletcher 1976: vol. 3, 510–11; 1.2.204–9)

This introduces a strain of qualified social realism into a play otherwise escapist. Indeed, one wonders whether the play's extreme emphasis on chastity is partly fuelled by a culturally rooted fear of venereal disease: in 5.3, that seems to be the Priest's suggestion expressed to Thenot:

> And like a glorious desperate man, that buies,
> A poison of much price, by which he dyes,
> Doest thou lay out for lust, whose only gaine,
> Is foule disease (Beaumont and Fletcher 1976: vol. 3, 569–70; 5.3.19–22)

Two main factors define tragicomic form for Fletcher: the intermingling of characters from different social strata with characters from different ontological spheres – gods, spirits, holy men, satyrs; and the possibility that characters can be brought close to death without compromising the happy final outcome. Blood is copiously shed. Alexis is wounded near to death by the Sullen Shepherd. Perigot wounds his lover Amoret not once but twice, the same Amoret who is thrown down a well! This leads Perigot to serious thoughts of suicide. To achieve the happy end, an elaborate plot is required deploying suspense and surprise to good effect, with reversals and recognitions aplenty. Although in *The Faithful Shepherdess* there are not the uncomfortably blended scenes that we have seen in Shakespeare's early tragicomedies, where the spectator is pulled in two directions simultaneously, Fletcher can change the mood and emotional temperature from scene to scene. And elements of tragicomic form that we have seen under development in Shakespeare are perceived and utilized by Fletcher. There are, for example, 'protector' figures who insure against the play's worst possibilities materializing – Clorin the herbalist, the River God and the Satyr. These are powerful forces ranged against the evil of the Sullen Shepherd and the nymphomaniacal plotting females Amarillis and Cloe.

Less suggestively Christian than Shakespearean tragicomedy, *The Faithful Shepherdess* is nevertheless obsessed with cleansing baptism. Amoret is rescued from the well by the River God at the end of Act 3. Incantatory rhyming tetrameter and song are the devices deployed to instil this with ritual significance. Shortly afterwards, in 4.2, the Satyr enters carrying the wounded Alexis, physically echoing the earlier rescue; and a cure effected by Clorin enacts a resurrection – all conducted in rhyming tetrameter. Immediately thereafter, Amarillis (who has plotted with the Sullen Shepherd to have Amoret thrown in the well) is struck by 'more than wonder, miracle!' to find her still alive. This is the 'hinge' that will gradually contrive the happy ending: 'the great powers will not let / Their verteous love be Crost' (Beaumont and Fletcher 1976: vol. 3, 554; 4.3.48–9) says a penitent and reforming Amarillis. That happy ending, however, has to wait because the nadir is not yet reached. The Sullen Shepherd's attempted rape of Amarillis and Perigot's soliloquy contemplating suicide in 4.4 are still to be overcome. After Perigot has wounded Amoret for the second time, he enters 'with his hand bloody' in 5.4. There follows a soliloquy drawing directly upon *Macbeth*, in which Perigot cannot cleanse his hand even with holy water: 'let these dew-dropps wash away my spot. / It will not cleanse, O to what sacred flood, / Shall I resort to wash away this blood' (Beaumont and Fletcher 1976: vol. 3, 574; 5.4.12–14). Thessalian society is poisoned at source by lust and by inflexible forms of chastity in equal measure. Unusually (and this perhaps contributed to the play's poor reception), it is the women who are sex-crazed and the men who are inflexibly chaste. The libidinal economy needs to be restored through the curative powers of Clorin (whose character might owe a debt to Helen in *All's Well*), through the white magic of the chastity test that counters the black magic of the poisoned well, and through the ritual exorcism of the Priest of Pan. As we have seen Shakespeare do in *Measure* and *All's Well*, this play deploys tetrameter passages and an extended use of music and song to bring about its ritualized social cleansing.

One can understand why its first audiences did not care for the play. It is not so much that they expected something raunchy and did not get it. A play in which Cloe can set up trysts with two lovers, Alexis and Daphnis, making her choice based on which one is the better sexual performer, and in which she can say 'It is Impossible to Ravish mee, / I am soe willing' (Beaumont and Fletcher 1976: vol. 3, 538; 3.1.212–13), is not a play lacking in erotic entertainment. It is more that the particular juxtaposition of innocence and experience, chastity and extreme sexual knowingness in the play, where the knowingness is mainly female and the chastity mainly male, must have disconcerted its initial audiences. A fetish is made out of chastity, insisted upon as the moral basis for all conduct. The single-mindedness of the play's obsession has Perigot attempting to murder his beloved Amoret twice because he thinks she is unchaste. The devout Clorin must pretend to have sexual desire for Thenot in order to ward him off. The Platonic Thenot loves Clorin for her very chastity, her devotion to her recently dead lover; he is disgusted by her love for a living being, even if that living being is himself! The play reduces itself to impotent adolescent sexual immaturity. As the Thenot and Clorin example suggests, Eros and Thanatos are uncomfortably intertwined in the action as characters draw each other's blood in the name of sexuality or chastity – here Fletcher is bringing his characters near death as his generic experiment demands that he should. But it produces an overall atmosphere of queasy unhealthiness. As in the Athens of *Midsummer Night's Dream*, Thessaly's libidinal economy has gone awry and magic is required to set it back to rights. Fletcher's play, though, takes itself a good deal more seriously than does Shakespeare's: no laughing comedy such as derives from Shakespeare's mechanicals ventilates its claustrophobic world.

Tragicomedy would enter the next phase of its development by means of another episode in the Fletcher/Shakespeare rivalry, when Fletcher collaborated with Francis Beaumont (1584/5–1616) in the writing of a play, *Philaster*, that impressed Shakespeare sufficiently to pick up some of its threads in his own *Cymbeline*. The writing team of Beaumont and Fletcher was successful enough to be engaged by the King's Men between 1610 and 1612, but as that collaboration began to weaken, Fletcher would have his sights set on Shakespeare as his new partner. Together, Shakespeare and Fletcher would write two tragicomedies, the lost *History of Cardenio* and *The Two Noble Kinsmen*. This embedding of tragicomedy is the subject of the next chapter.

2

A Genre Established: Tragicomedy 1610–42

Re-enter Fletcher and Shakespeare: *Philaster* and *Cymbeline*

Although we no longer think of Shakespeare as an isolated genius composing somewhere in the stratosphere, the idea of him gaining inspiration from rival playwrights can still surprise us. Such emulation occurs again in 1609–10, when Beaumont and Fletcher's tragicomedy *Philaster* was staged, providing Shakespeare with several hints towards his own *Cymbeline*. These two plays move the form away from satire, diluting though not altogether forsaking the pastoral elements, towards romantic tragicomedy. Valerie Wayne's account in her recent Arden edition of *Cymbeline* of all the elements that have gone into Shakespeare's extraordinary mix (Shakespeare 2017: 94–109) shows that some plot elements have specific sources, but that Shakespeare drew upon a surprising range of literary works and authors, including prominent Roman writers Virgil and Ovid, and near-contemporaries such as Sidney, Spenser, Beaumont and Fletcher, Camden, Speed, Montaigne and Cervantes. Beyond that, though, there is an entire landscape of ancient Greek romances translated into English in the sixteenth century. The plot of *Philaster* is shaped out of *The Faithful Shepherdess* and an earlier Beaumont and Fletcher play *Cupid's Revenge*. More generally, many plot elements that feature in both *Philaster* and *Cymbeline* are of ancient and folk-tale origin. Specifically, both plays share a wronged, calumniated heiress, both have the transvestite female motif (Bellario, Philaster's page, is actually the absconded Euphrasia, just as Innogen spends some of the action disguised as a page boy, Fidele), both use elements derived from Court masques to bring about the dénouement and they share a source in misogynistic quotation from Juvenal's *Satire VI*. In some ways most striking (if one pardons the pun) is that, in both plays, the heroine is wounded by the man who supposedly loves her. We have seen that violence inflicted upon women by their lovers features in Guarini, in Fletcher's *Faithful Shepherdess* and now again in the tragicomedies of 1609–10. Physical violence, the wounding near to death of a female character by a male in breach of any chivalric code, is one means through which tragicomedy takes its characters as close to a tragic fate as the form can permit. This repositioning of women, the woman given her death-wound, becomes a characteristic of tragicomedy. It offers wider possibilities for acting female roles.

By 1610, tragicomedy has become a framing device, a means of shaping disparate material from folk, romance and historico-literary sources into a pattern that is commanding increasing audience recognition and approval. *Philaster* illustrates this shaping clearly. From the outset, the action is focalized through the eyes of three cynical, worldly commentators, the Sicilian gentlemen Dion, Cleremont and Thrasiline. Apart from their expository function of telling us things we need to know – that the King is marrying his daughter (Arethusa) to a Spanish prince (Pharamond) despite the fact that the genuine heir to the throne (Philaster) is still living at court, loves her and has much popular support – these commentators are used to puncture some of the main-plot rhetoric and, in scenes with tragic potential, to deflect some of that into a different, comic key. This happens most obviously in 4.4, when the King enters in search of his missing daughter, blustering, fulminating and demanding that Dion tell him where she is:

> **King.** I do command you all, as you are subjects,
> To show her me! What, am I not your King?
> If ay, then am I not to be obeyed?
>
> **Dion.** Yes, if you command things possible and honest.
>
> **King.** Things possible and honest? Hear me, thou,
> Thou traitor, thou darest confine thy King to things
> Possible and honest! Show her me ...
>
> **Dion.** Faith, I cannot, unless you tell me where she is. (Beaumont and Fletcher 2009: 4.4.32–8; 41)

The King produces further rhetoric in this vein, to the effect that, as king, he is able to control the elements: 'whose breath can still the winds ... Speak, can it not?' To this, Dion gives a blunt single-word answer, 'No', going on to comment on his bad breath. Royal dignity scarcely survives this exchange.

But from the outset, *Philaster* fails to take its characters entirely seriously. Pharamond, the Spanish prince, is introduced making a fatuous self-congratulatory speech to the effect that he is the answer to the Sicilian kingdom's dreams: a speech Cleremont calls 'a large inventory of his own commendations' that, apart from confirming every anti-Spanish prejudice of the Blackfriars audience, ensures that he will never be a true contender for the Princess Arethusa's heart. As is the pattern in tragicomedy, villains and heroes are more difficult to distinguish than they are in tragedy. Philaster's psychological state is heavily modelled on that of Hamlet. Infused with his dead, usurped father's spirit, Philaster's state of possession appears in the riddling cast of his speech. As the play develops, Philaster is to act in an anti-heroic, even cowardly fashion, that will test to the limits the audience's desire to take him to their hearts. Yet perhaps the play's characters are being remote-controlled.

Figure 5 *Priscilla Hopkins as Arethusa in Fletcher's* Philaster *performed at Drury Lane theatre in 1773. Engraved by Thornthwaite after an illustration by James Roberts from* Bell's British Theatre *(1778). Hopkins later married the leading actor John Philip Kemble. Photo by Florilegius/Alamy Stock Photo.*

When Arethusa declares her love for him, with a forwardness upon which Philaster comments, she introduces the theme of divine dispensation: 'the secret justice of the gods' is manifest in their love.

Sidney, Spenser and Guarini are summoned in a pastoral idyll conjured up by Philaster to explain how he came by his page, Bellario, whom he now offers to Arethusa as a go-between (1.2.112–40). Bellario represents the pastoral virtues of innocence and unstinting loyalty, but in the softness of his speech and the pure ardency of his sentiments, what is culturally marked as effeminacy shows through the male attire (always already complicated by the use of boy actors). Philaster becomes convinced that Bellario has become Arethusa's lover, a conviction not shared by the audience that senses a certain as yet unplaceable gender-perplexity. Contemporaries were well-attuned to such sexualized ambiguities from Shakespearean comedy and pastoral. A scene in which Bellario's devotion to Philaster is demonstrated is followed by a bawdy scene (2.2) where the newly betrothed Pharamond's sexual frustration emerges through a quibble on 'country ladies', familiar from *Hamlet*. He tries unsuccessfully to bed one court lady, then transfers his attention to another, Megra, who has taken an unaccountably ill-judged fancy to him and will shortly circulate rumours concerning Arethusa and Bellario. Old-fashioned pastoral fealty is thus juxtaposed with Pharamond's utter lack of it in the context of the court. Thus, the plaiting of noble, high-minded and uplifting scenes with low and bawdy sex comedy continues. Hints that the King is not an unregenerate villain are thrown out towards the close of Act 2, when in soliloquy he betrays his troubled conscience – more echoes of *Hamlet*. That interiorized scene is followed by the King's discovery of Pharamond and Megra *in flagrante*. Embarrassed by this evidence of his future son-in-law's worthlessness, the King addresses Megra in time-honoured misogynistic terms ('Thou most ill-shrouded rottenness, thou piece / Made by a painter and a 'pothecary' [2.4.135–6]), but she wipes the floor with him, accusing Arethusa of equivalent dishonour. The King does not come out even, much less on top. The act ends with Dion again speaking the audience's puzzlement and suspicion that things are not what they seem.

In Act 3, the central confrontation between Philaster and Bellario takes a direction typically tragicomic. Philaster tries to winkle out of Bellario evidence that he has seen his mistress naked: 'Are not her breasts two liquid ivory balls?' (3.1.212). Reminiscent of *Othello* and anticipatory of Iachimo's inspection of Innogen's naked body in *Cymbeline*, the action departs from tragedy because Bellario immediately sees through this to the root of the problem, concluding at once that his master has been 'abused' by 'some villain'. His innocence, his unquestioning loyalty even to one who has drawn a sword upon him, his willingness to die rather than to traduce his mistress's reputation: all of this acts as a kind of magical protection, a guarantee that he will not be hewn into pieces by a furious Philaster. The word 'service' echoes and re-echoes, toggling between its chivalrous meaning and its sexual undertone, as the play's protagonists struggle to decide which of those two forms of 'service' they are called upon to perform. Here again, Philaster's posturing borders on the comic:

> **Phi.** False Arethusa!
> Hast thou a medicine to restore my wits,
> When I have lost 'em? If not, leave to talk,
> And do thus.
>
> **Are.** Do what, sir? Would you sleep?
>
> (3.2.99–102)

As the Revels editor Andrew Gurr notes, Philaster must here be closing his eyes to simulate death, but the pathos is more tragicomic than tragic because Arethusa doesn't quite 'get' it, leaving Philaster looking ridiculous (Beaumont and Fletcher 1973: 66).

Act 4 is an extended experiment in tragicomic mingling of characters from different social strata, with some unexpected results. Dion's blunt puncturing of the King's ego has already been noticed, but before that happens in 4.4, other confrontations between nobility and commoners have taken place. The action moves outdoors, to the hunt. No one looks more ridiculous than the postcoital Pharamond, described by Dion as 'an old surfeited stallion after his leaping, dull as a dormouse' (4.1.6–7). The three gentlemen maintain a bawdy comic commentary on the King and the Spanish prince, ensuring that the audience retains no respect for them. Bawdy comedy continues with two woodmen who discuss the sexual availability of the court ladies, Megra coming top of the league: 'That's a firker i'faith, boy ... She rides well and she pays well' (4.2.25, 31–2). Philaster enters, raging against women in terms borrowed from Juvenal's sixth satire, a misogynistic posture that will be directly contradicted by Bellario's dedication – later, when Bellario's true identity is discovered. Dion questions the woodmen on whether they have seen Arethusa and they, despite their seemingly helpful questions ('Was she not young and tall?') snub him: 'Faith, my Lord, we saw none.' This device, of rustics scoring points at the expense of courtiers, is one that Fletcher enjoyed and is used in his later writing. The tone is raised again as Philaster, Arethusa and Bellario encounter one another and in a bewildering series of passionate reversals, Philaster begs Arethusa to take his life, but instead wounds her, whereupon '*Enter a* Country Fellow', who adopts the chivalrous stance vacated by his social superior Philaster, immediately rushing to Arethusa's aid. Although this is a combat that Philaster would expect to win, the Country Fellow is a 'protector' figure, quasi-supernaturally endowed with strength:

> **Phi.** I am hurt,
> The gods take part against me, could this boor
> Have held me thus else?
>
> (4.5.102–4)

The world is turned upside down to such an extent that only divine providence can account for it. The play reaches its nadir in 4.6 when against all chivalric regulations Philaster wounds Bellario while s/he is asleep. Bellario's immediate concern for Philaster's well-being betokens the power of selfless forgiveness that, in tragicomedy of this period, is the social healing agent that will bring about a happy ending.

In the final act, the writers are feeling their way with the new tragicomic mode. How many more obstacles should there be to delay the happy ending? How late in the play can they afford to retain the possibility that the play will end in death? Arethusa, Bellario and Philaster are now all imprisoned and the discussion is of forgiveness and resignation unto death. At this point the three prisoners present a marriage masque, a daring piece of staging that recalls the masque written by Ben Jonson in 1606 for the marriage of the Earl of Essex and Lady Frances Howard, *Hymenaei*. In this way, the public theatre was able to smuggle in performative elements usually restricted to the court. Here Bellario, impersonating Hymen the god of marriage, declares Arethusa and Philaster to be actually married. Anticipating Jupiter's descent in *Cymbeline*, the imagery maps a natural rhythm onto the tragicomic shaping structure: of the pair as 'two fair cedar branches' whose beauty has been choked by 'shrubs, / Base underbrambles ... brakes, rude thorns and thistles' (5.3.25–44). The King, however, turns this erotic moment into metatheatrical dust:

> I'll provide a masque shall make
> Your Hymen turn his saffron into a sullen coat,
> And sing sad requiems to your departing souls.
> (5.3.53–5)

A new sonority is heard from now onwards through the ensuing popular uprising orchestrated by the three Sicilian gentlemen, retailed in demotic language that contrasts starkly with Philaster's high rhetoric. Penitence is now the dominant tone of the King's rhetoric: his enlisting of Philaster's aid to quell the insurgents might be a faint echo of *Coriolanus*. Act 5, Scene 4 is a crowd-pleasing scene devoted to giving Pharamond an anti-Spanish skimmington ride, as a Captain and several rebel citizens terrify him with the prospect of dismemberment. Philaster himself puts a stop to this rough treatment, showing the noble forgiveness that in tragicomedy restores the social bond. Megra's malice towards the Princess, continuing the accusation that she has played false with Bellario, is confuted in a *coup de théâtre*. Bellario is revealed to be Dion's lost daughter Euphrasia, a woman and so incapable of betraying Philaster. She returns from a self-imposed pilgrimage undertaken on account of her hopeless love for Philaster. Her restoration is a reward for her father's protective role, his suspicion of Bellario now appropriately ironized.

Does this play – does the genre itself – have a politics? The argument that it does has certainly been made. My own view is that tragicomedies are written so as not to deal *directly* with contemporary political events, but to *resonate* with them. The insurgency in *Philaster* might allude to the Midlands food riots of 1607–8 that form a background to another King's Men play of 1608, Shakespeare's *Coriolanus*. Its action must have called to mind the secret marriage of the King's cousin Arbella Stuart to William Seymour, while the confrontation between the King and Dion noticed above resonates with, and reverses the outcome of, the facing down of Lord Chief Justice Coke by King James over the extent of royal prerogative that erupted on 13 November 1608. *Cymbeline* is obsessively concerned with Britishness and, like *Philaster*, has a sprinkling of detail that does seem to be specifically identifiable with offstage events. But as its Arden editor Suzanne Gossett shows, *Philaster* was revived as and when its plot seemed to echo political events (Beaumont and Fletcher 2009: 33–41). In Fletcher's hands, tragicomic form had reusable potential. *Philaster*'s very absence of specific detail made for a longer shelf life. In Shakespeare's hands, as I hope to show by means of an analysis of *The Winter's Tale*, tragicomic form could take on important religious and metaphysical questions beyond the political.

The Winter's Tale and the Metaphysics of Tragicomedy

In the previous chapter, we noted that Aristotle allowed for the possibility that tragedy could end happily. He had to, because he knew of examples of such ambivalent plays – in particular Euripides' *Alcestis* (438 BCE). Translated into Latin by George Buchanan and performed before Queen Elizabeth in the 1560s, the play was well enough known in Shakespeare's time for him to have read it and a grammar school education was sufficient to deal with the Latin. John Pitcher, editor of the Arden Third Series edition of *The Winter's Tale*, considers *Alcestis* an important shaping influence on the play's conception of romantic tragicomedy (Shakespeare 2010: 12–13). In *Alcestis*, King Admetus has been granted life beyond death by Apollo, but on condition that he finds a substitute when the day of his death arrives. His dutiful wife Alcestis agrees to sacrifice herself for him. Apollo and Thanatos (Death) quarrel, the former prophesying that a man will come who would wrestle Alcestis out of Death's hands. This man proves to be Admetus' old friend Heracles (Hercules). Alcestis appears actually to die, but when Heracles offers to Admetus a veiled woman as a new partner, the lifted veil reveals the woman to be Alcestis. The relevance of this model to a play whose heroine appears to return from the dead is not far to seek.

Probably begun in 1610 and finished early in 1611, *Winter's Tale* seems deliberately to eschew contemporary allusion, offering instead a canvas for the playing out of large mythical patterns. Resurrection – almost a constituting convention of tragicomedy as we have seen – is the most significant of those. Perdita alludes to the classical resurrection myth of Persephone under the Latin name Proserpina in the flower ritual that she performs in Act 4. The young Persephone was collecting flowers near Enna, in Sicily, when she was dragged off by Hades into the lower world. Since she went through a form of marriage there, she was obliged to spend one-third of her time with Hades, her mother Demeter insisting that the rest of her time should be spent in the upper world, helping her goddess-mother who presided over the fertility of the earth. Hence Persephone is emblematic of vegetable life that comes and goes with the changing seasons. In spring, when the seeds sprout up from the ground, she rises to her mother; in winter, after the harvest, she returns to her subterranean kingdom as the seed returns to the dark grave of the earth. From this notion of dark and light, death and life, burial and resurrection, the Persephone myth becomes an image of immortality that lies at the heart of ancient mystery cults known as the Eleusinian mysteries. *The Winter's Tale* treats such material in a way that moves it closer to Christianity and to the Resurrection upon which Christian faith is grounded. *The Winter's Tale* exceeds John Fletcher's brief for tragicomedy cited earlier in that it allows a character, Mamillius, actually to die. It is therefore a more radical experiment in audience manipulation. Rather than being asked to come back from the brink of the grave, we are asked to climb out of it, to resurrect.

Tragicomedies are sometimes thought to be tragic, then comic. Readers of this book may be persuaded, however, that this is not usually how they work. Certainly the prevailing 'generic mood' created by plot events and discourse will be darker in the early action and lighter in the late, but *The Winter's Tale* develops the art of the blended scene to its highest expression in the drama of the period. Perhaps no single scene to be found anywhere in tragicomedy provides a better example of tragicomic blend than *The Winter's Tale* 3.3. Antigonus is operating on Leontes' cruel instruction to abandon Leontes' baby daughter somewhere and let her take her chances of survival. Since Leontes was for some time resolved upon *burning* the child, audiences becoming adept at identifying tragicomic signals would recognize that this relative clemency offers at least the possibility of a happier outcome. Antigonus's entrance, carrying the baby, makes for great pathos. He has had a vivid dream, or if his Protestant faith would permit it, he has seen Hermione's ghost: 'I have heard, but not believed, the spirits of the dead / May walk again' (3.3.15–16). The effect on an audience is paradoxical: they are kept in mind of Hermione, but if her spirit is Antigonus's messenger, then it is surely proof that she is dead? And the ghost is shooting the messenger. Antigonus will not live, because he has been appointed the 'thrower-out' of the baby: 'most accursed am I / To be by oath enjoined to this' (51–2). Harshly expressed by the neologism 'thrower out', Antigonus's blighted function might be in the tradition of Greek drama, but it engages an audience's sense of fair play. 'That's not fair' is likely to be a modern audience's reaction. There follows the most famous stage direction in all of Shakespeare: *Exit, pursued by a bear.* Much ink has been spilled on the question of how this was staged; whether by a real bear, as has been proposed because the bear garden was adjacent to the Globe and because there were celebrated trained bears, or by a man in a bear suit. In modern staging, lighting and sound effects can do the job. An already uneasy audience can be manipulated in the direction of pathos or of farce.

The entrance of the Shepherd and Clown can be read as the moment when winter gives place to spring in the play, resurrection/regeneration as figured in the Persephone myth. This is indicated by the Shepherd's lines that directors must be tempted to etch on the production merchandise: 'thou met'st with things dying, I with things newborn' (110–11). Here is a tragicomic 'hinge' if ever there was one. Those lines, though, are like a musical cadence, a resolution of much discordant material. The Shepherd's discovery of the baby is rendered in the language of sexual mishap: 'some stair-work, some trunk-work, some behind-door-work' (72–3). Queasier, even, than this traduction is the Clown's description of the shipwreck, the drowning of the mariners and the consumption of Antigonus by the bear. As the Clown offers his eye-witness testimony of those events, the audience is wondering whether he might not have been better deployed going to Antigonus's aid. The simpletonian matter-of-factness – 'I'll go see if the bear be gone from the gentleman, and how much he hath eaten' (125–7) – juxtaposed with the rustics' gloating over the finding of what they take to be fairy gold, is challengingly melded dramatic material.

But indeed the play has been challenging from the outset. Unlike Othello who has reason to be jealous, Leontes lives in a solipsistic world not shared by any other courtier. Again unlike *Othello*, *Winter's Tale* does not concern itself with psychological probing even if some of the imagery suggests a kind of arrested development or unhealthily prolonged childhood as a reason for Leontes' sexual paranoia. In later tragicomedy, especially in Fletcher's hands, the psychological probing of the mind tends to be displaced onto the machinery of a complex plot. We do better to understand the play's opening as a fairy tale *donnée*. 'Once upon a time there was a jealous tyrant called Leontes.' If we tell our children a story that begins 'once upon a time there was a wicked witch', we expect instant buy-in, rather than a series of questions about how the witch came to be wicked. Dangerous though it clearly is, there is nevertheless something irresistibly comic in the way Leontes expresses his jealousy:

> There have been,
> Or I am much deceived, cuckolds ere now,
> And many a man there is even at this present,
> Now, while I speak this, holds his wife by th'arm,
> That little thinks she has been sluiced in's absence,
> And his pond fished by his next neighbour, by
> Sir Smile, his neighbour.
>
> (1.2.189–95)

If, as the lines seem to demand, this speech is taken directly to the audience, it is going to draw them into an uncomfortable cuckold's concord with Leontes; rather than bonding the disparate individuals of an audience into a greater unity, as theatre so often seeks to do, this speech divides the audience into suspicious monads, each turning uncertainly to look at the man standing or sitting next to him. Leontes' assumption that the world is comprised of cuckolds and their faithless partners, which he invites the audience to share again in the 'Inch-thick, knee-deep' speech (1.2.185–206), is simultaneously frighteningly persuasive and comically ridiculous.

Act 2, Scene 3 is fascinating from the point of view of tragicomedy. Paulina enters here with Leontes' newborn child, determined to shock the father out of his paranoiac world view by demonstrating the unmistakeable resemblance between his child and himself. The stakes are high. Yet the scene is ambushed for an entirely different topos: that of the henpecked husband. As both Camillo and Antigonus fail to rein in Paulina's lashing tongue, Leontes taunts the other men with their inability to control a woman: 'Antigonus, / I charged thee that she should not come about me. / I knew she would' (41–3); 'What, canst not rule her?' (45); 'He dreads his wife' (78). He isn't having much success himself, but that observation seems to escape him. Thus a scene that one would expect to be high on pathos actually becomes a comic variation on an old theme, the hagridden husband. It prepares the way for the solemn and dignified scene of Hermione's trial (3.2), another scene that undercuts its would-be stage-manager Leontes. This cannot but recall and resonate with historical trials in which women have figured – that of Katherine of Aragon, of Anne Boleyn and, in 1587, of Mary Stuart, Queen of Scots. As in those prior cases, tyrannical and wrongful accusations are rebutted by a queen fully in control of her emotions and rhetoric. Even in Shakespeare there is little to rival the lines (3.2.89–114) in which Hermione takes the ground from under Leontes' feet by telling him that his love is her *raison d'être* and, having lost it, she has no more reason to live. After the disclosure of the oracle and the sacrificial death of Mamillius, repentance is immediately introduced as a theme.

In other tragicomedies upon which we have focused, there have been choric passages marked by rhyming couplet verse. So there is in *The Winter's Tale*, where Time enters as an apologist for a radical breach of the unities of time and place, delivering a speech in sixteen rhyming couplets that steps out of the 'realistic' frame, asking the audience to take leaps of faith. The chorus renews the contract between performers and audience: awake your faith in our tale. Experimentation continues in Act 4, which reverts to the pastoral form favoured by Beaumont and Fletcher – but in the character of Autolycus, it puts a real toad in the imaginary garden. Seldom can a new character have made such an explosive entrance. It is as if Autolycus (the name means 'lone wolf') has wandered off the set of one of Ben Jonson's city comedies, to find himself part of a pastoral idyll where simple country rustics provide him with rich pickings. His presence ensures that this version of pastoral never is idyllic; indeed, his bid for the Clown's sympathy is an ironic reversal of the Good Samaritan parable. Even the long and beautiful pastoral scene, 4.4, with its strains of song, dance and masque, is not idyllic. When Florizel's father Polixenes offers to 'have thy beauty scratched with briars, / And made more homely than thy state' (4.4.430–1), Perdita can see how he will turn the country plants that she loves into weapons of defamation and torture. Autolycus's later encounter with the Clown recapitulates that between William and Touchstone in *As You Like It*. Innate worth pitted against the often-specious merits of social rank is the focus both of this encounter and of the scene as a whole. It runs through the highly emblematic discourse about flower-grafting and underprops Polixenes's conviction that Perdita must be worthless because she is not ostensibly nobly born (Figure 6). Tragicomic pastoral has been a vehicle for examination of the nature/nurture debate since Guarini.

The final act commences. Cleomenes, a Sicilian lord, addresses Leontes (5.1.1–6) stating the themes of the act. Sorrow – penitence – redemption – forgiveness: this pattern has featured in earlier tragicomedy but never has it been so magnificently demonstrated. Perdita is restored to her father in a reported scene that, along with the oracle and its prophecy and the allusion to the Alcestis story, emphasizes the Greek elements of the play. In the final scene, Paulina is going to stage-manage a resurrection: a statue is going to come to life before the very eyes of a small onstage audience. As noted, the

Figure 6 *Richard Cosway's painting of Mary Robinson playing the role of Perdita in* The Winter's Tale, *c.1779. In this role, she captivated the Prince of Wales (future George IV) and began a notorious career as a celebrity mistress, and later a poet and novelist. Photo by Heritage Art/Heritage Images via Getty Images.*

larger audience has been given clues that Hermione is not to be forgotten, alongside clues that she is dead: they do not know what is true. On an analogy with the aesthetic viewing of a particularly lifelike statue in a gallery, but with an irresistible parallel to theatrical performance, the royal party visits Paulina's house where she '*draws a curtain*'. Awestruck wonder is the immediate reaction: the same 'wonder' that we have seen it to be the objective of tragicomic drama to provoke. She seems to prevent Leontes from kissing the statue and marring its fresh paint. Here, there seem to be two dangers: the invasion of the space between viewer and viewed, so as to threaten the illusion, and a form of idol-worship. Referring to beliefs such as Purgatory as a realm inhabited by ghosts, this play has already flirted with Catholicism. So it seems to be doing again in the final act. Paulina is concerned to secure her audience's credentials: 'Either forbear, / Quit presently the chapel ... But then you'll think – / Which I protest against – I am assisted / By wicked powers'; 'It is required / You do awake your faith'; 'Or those that think it is unlawful business / I am about, let them depart'; 'Her actions shall be holy as / You hear my spell is lawful' (5.3.85–104). Extreme Protestants – Puritans – would not buy into theatrical illusion and religious extremists might indeed think that this stage action is a travesty of Christian mysteries. But as Paulina calls for music and choreographically leads Hermione down from her podium, Leontes vindicates the power of theatre: 'If this be magic, let it be an art / Lawful as eating' (5.3.109–10). That is what has been at stake – the power of theatre to convince an audience that they have seen a miracle. The play issues a caveat to would-be performers: beware of a poor performance because the audience will not believe in the play.

Shakespeare's appropriation of romantic tragicomedy in *The Winter's Tale* is designed, I believe, to carve out a particular metaphysical space. This is what we may term the metaphysics of the 'second chance'. In life, we are not often given the opportunity to atone for our serious errors; but art can offer us that chance. Through the manifestation of divine intervention, or through less embodied, more mystical procedures, the audience for Shakespeare's late plays is given the comfort of knowing that human errors, however serious and potentially tragic, will not necessarily realize their worst-case scenarios. Time's inexorability, irresistible in tragedy, is resisted in a play such as *The Winter's Tale* through what we might think to be actual embodiment as a character. Faulty and weak human beings such as Leontes can be given the opportunity, through being brought face to face with their crimes and expressing penitence, to redeem time: through processes of generational repair in *The Winter's Tale* (and in *Pericles* and *The Tempest*) to effect a symbolic reversal of time. Characters seemingly dead can actually come to life, can resurrect to enable a second chance in the most literal and at the same time metaphysical of ways. That, in Shakespeare's hands, is what tragicomedy can offer.

John Fletcher: The Genius of Tragicomedy

Although we have nailed our colours to the mast in arguing that *The Winter's Tale* was the genre's greatest achievement pre-1642, Shakespeare's masterpiece would not become the post-1660 'template' tragicomedy. Whereas in the 1630s London theatre was taking on a commercial bias, with rival groups of actors soliciting the custom of relatively disparate audiences, its restoration would be tightly controlled by two, and only two, royal patents granted to courtiers Thomas Killigrew and William Davenant to operate in only two theatre buildings. In the immediate aftermath of the theatres reopening in the 1659–60 season, Killigrew's King's Company had taken over a group of experienced actors from the Red Bull Theatre, enjoying the performance rights to pre-Restoration plays. Davenant's younger Duke's troupe taken over from the Phoenix Theatre had nothing to perform until a petition to the Lord Chamberlain produced a warrant on 12 December 1660, giving him exclusive rights to eleven plays, including nine of Shakespeare's. Revivals of pre-1642 plays soon tailed off, however, as those were perceived to be unsuited to sophisticated, Frenchified tastes. Exiled in Paris for several years, Charles II was determined, after his coronation in 1660, to reinstitute theatre as a reflection of a French-inspired courtly culture. Many of Shakespeare's plays that were performed (*The Winter's Tale* not amongst them) were performed in radically altered form, as the case study of Nahum Tate's version of *Lear* in the next chapter discusses.

The two pre-1642 plays most frequently revived after 1660 were both by John Fletcher and were both tragicomedies: *The Humorous Lieutenant*, written *c.*1619, and *The Island Princess*, given its first recorded performance on 26 December 1621 and probably written between 1619 and 1621 but not in print before 1647. *The Island Princess* had elements that made it unacceptable to audiences in its original form and it was always presented as an adaptation. It has many kinds of fascination very well discussed by Clare McManus, the Arden editor of the text; and it is to that edition that readers eager to find out more about the play in context should turn (Fletcher 2017). I will confine my comments to some brief remarks about genre: how did contemporary spectators decode it and how did the play in performance structure its own reception? An initial observation is that the metaphysical dimension of a play such as *The Winter's Tale* is at best skeletal in Fletcher. Fortune is this play's presiding deity, which in practice means vagaries, twists and turns. If in *Winter's Tale* there are 'protector' figures such as Antigonus, Camillo and Paulina, whom the spectator trusts to bring about a happy outcome, the signposting of *The Island Princess* is more obscure. Tragicomedy, we have said, tries to do justice to the complexity of experience. In this play, that means unpredictability: heroes and villains are difficult to tell apart to the extent that heroes can turn into villains and vice versa. Character appears to serve story. If telling a rattling good yarn means that characters must behave inconsistently, then so be it. Repentance figures prominently as we have seen that it does in earlier tragicomedies – characters several times express regret over their actions – but in Fletcher's hands this is not part of a larger pattern such as is Shakespeare's metaphysics of the second chance.

Fletcher's concern in this tragicomedy is to vindicate the Christian faith: specifically, even though the Christians are Portuguese, to vindicate Protestantism. The play builds to a climactic scene (4.5) in which the princess Quisara, a Moslem, requires that her Portuguese inamorato Armusia convert to Islam. In Fletcher's hands, however, the version of Islam presented has not a shred of authenticity. It is a pagan-Catholic confection, so that the ensuing struggle between the Moslem characters and the Christians comes to resonate with contemporary anti-Catholic rhetoric. By extreme sleight of hand, the Portuguese appear as Protestants while the language used of the Moslems is suggestive of Catholic religious practice. Act 4, Scene 5 resembles the 'Kill Claudio' *coup de théâtre* in *Much Ado* 4.1. Quisara has one further challenge for Armusia to meet before she will bestow her heart:

> **Quisara** I'll tell you then: change your religion
> And be of one belief with me. (Fletcher 2017: 4.5.33–4)

Armusia, horrified, claims that Quisara's religion worships dogs and cats and 'every bird that flies and every worm' (42). In an emotional speech (73–95), he draws a distinction between worshipping the sun and moon and worshipping the creator of those celestial objects, moving into accusations that, in their coded reference to the Catholic mystery of transubstantiation, are obvious anti-Catholic slurs, even anticipating the icon-smashing of militant Protestants during the Civil War. Two central characters in the play, the princess Quisara herself and the Portuguese adventurer that she uses to bring about her purposes, Pinheiro, are morally ambiguous. Their actions stem more from the exigencies of the adventure story than from any more consistent psychological basis.

The Humorous Lieutenant was played much as Fletcher wrote it. It did not present equivalent thematic challenges, nor did it have such potential to offend. There is a degree of separation between the material pursued in its serious plot and the comic underplot – an incipient 'double-plot' structure that John Dryden would pick up and develop. This play was very popular post-1660, many times revived. Dryden could have seen it performed in every season up to 1663. Regular productions occur until the late 1760s, with adaptations thereafter, making it the period's most popular tragicomedy. What characteristics account for its perennial popularity?

Set in Greece in the post-Alexandrine period, the main plot has King Antigonus, described as '*an old Man with young desires*', at war with three rival kings who have shared out Alexander the Great's territories. His son Demetrius is eager to be blooded in combat, but his first forays into battle fail. He is forced to flee, leaving comrades behind. His honour is dealt a second blow when the rival kings, impressed by Demetrius's brave actions, show clemency to his captured troops. That debt of honour is paid off when Demetrius later offers peace terms to the monarchs that involve no forfeitures of their lands. Out of this courtesy plot radiate two other actions. In the first, a young woman, Celia, has been captured by Antigonus's army after a siege at Antioch. Captivated by her beauty and virtue, Demetrius has ransomed her and she is now in his protection. Intending to try her suitability for the Prince's hand, Antigonus orders his network of pimps and bawds to lure Celia to his court, but he soon falls in love with her himself. Father and son become suitors to the same woman. Antigonus's lust is withered by Celia's supernal virtue, and he concedes her to his son, but not before he has misinformed his son of her death. 'Resurrected' and restored to Demetrius, Celia takes a méchante revenge by pretending that she has been successfully seduced at Court, a story that Demetrius believes. He reacts by assuring her that she is dead to him:

> thou art dead indeed, lost, tainted;
> … Thou art dead, for ever dead; sins surfeit slew thee
> (Beaumont and Fletcher 1982: vol. 5, 394–5; 4.8.80, 86)

She in turn is disgusted that he can doubt her faith; Demetrius's 'minder' Leontius is required to orchestrate a rapprochement, stage-managed rather as Leontes and Hermione's reunion is by Paulina in *Winter's Tale*.

In the second radiating action, the eponymous Lieutenant is a preternaturally courageous fighter, a kind of secret weapon who can vanquish many opponents at once, provided he is kept in a painful condition that results from his having the pox. He is 'humorous' not in the modern sense, but in the seventeenth-century sense of being inflamed by choleric 'humours' resulting from excess blood. When his blood is let on the battlefield, he resorts to his natural condition – a Falstaffian brand of cowardice. In his more anaemic conditions, the Lieutenant has no more time for warfare, courage and other military values than does Shakespeare's fat knight. The comic subplot results from the ebb and flow of the Lieutenant's blood supply, and the manipulation of his temperament by his fellow-soldiers, who at one point persuade him that his illness has returned and that he must return to the battlefield to be bled. At another, they designate the Lieutenant to be the emissary to the crazed and violent Demetrius, again because, in his agonized state, he alone has the 'courage' to face him. The Lieutenant's final indignity results from accidentally consuming a magic philtre prepared on the King's behalf and intended for Celia. Falling crazily in love with the King, the Lieutenant spends much of his later time in the play collecting royal souvenirs and otherwise manifesting his bizarrely induced passion for Antigonus.

The Humorous Lieutenant has many of the features that define tragicomedy for the new post-1660 generation of theatregoers and dramatists, features that Restoration playwrights such as John Dryden needed to adapt to emerging canons of taste. Notable here is the intermingling of a court-world in which behaving with nobility, courtesy and honour is the supreme value, and a world of prostitutes, pimps and procuresses that serves the venereal needs of the courtiers. Three servants, Timon, Charinthus and Menippus, are employed in servicing the King's vices. Their most reliable source of young women, the bawd Leucippe, is represented practising her trade, bringing into prostitution a country girl called Phoebe. That world of sexually transmitted disease informs the lieutenant subplot: his ersatz courage results from syphilitic agony. The play's imagery is heavily dominated by olfactory unpleasantness. It is a landscape of stink and smell. Perhaps the closest we have come to this is the darkly poisonous atmosphere of Shakespeare's *Measure for Measure*. The leading couple, Demetrius and Celia, struggle to rise above this miasma, without total success. Celia is bought by the prince and must endure his father's attempt to repurchase her. Fletcher's early tragicomic mission, to intermingle high-life and low-life characters, was never more fully accomplished than in this play. In some respects, this would be too strong a diet for post-1660 audiences; in others, though, they would develop even stronger stomachs, particularly for sexual titillation – as we will discuss in regard to Dryden's tragicomedies in the next chapter.

Memes that we have come to associate with tragicomedy recur here. Early on, the brave veteran Leontius is assigned to Demetrius as a protector figure, a function he discharges honourably throughout the entire action. Celia's supraworldly virtue will suggest to those who know their tragicomedy that she is not the poor slave that she appears – and indeed, she is revealed as Enanthe, daughter of the rival king Seleucus, in the final scene. Before her identity is revealed, she has to undergo a symbolic death, declared dead to Demetrius, which offers the opportunity for symbolic resurrection, a memetic feature of tragicomedy. She is declared to be a 'wonder' (5.4.38), cueing in the awestruck astonishment that tragicomic dénouements hope to conjure in their audiences. Typical of tragicomedy's feisty female protagonists, Celia wipes the floor with Antigonus's attempt to seduce her:

> Your will's a poore one;
> And though it be a King's will, a despised one,
> Weaker then Infants leggs, your will's in swadling clouts:

A thousand waies my will has found to checke ye;
A thousand doores to scape ye. (Beaumont and Fletcher 1982: vol. 5, 388; 4.5.60–4)

She will later trounce her fiancé Demetrius to the same extent. Intergenerational conflict is sharply focused through the direct and incestuously queasy father–son rivalry featured in the plot. And if the sexualized world of Fletcher's Greece is represented with a degree of realism, nevertheless the power of magic is not eschewed. As a magician prepares the love-philtre in 4.3, his song conjures up '*an Antick of little* Fayeries' who dance around the bowl, adding ingredients including '*a little little Flower*' and '*the powder of the Moone*'. A catalogue of charms successful in provoking love in ancient myth is added to the brew. Song, dance, spectacle, magic, mythology: Fletcher bakes those tragicomic ingredients using his own recipe.

This is the tragicomedy, then, that was most frequently revived post-1660 and thus came to represent tragicomedy in the pre-closure era. Its influence would be reflected through the prism of French neoclassical aesthetics. The direction taken by English tragicomedy would be heavily influenced by the success of Pierre Corneille's dramatic career and in particular his play *Le Cid* (1637). No dramatist caused more 'anxiety of influence' for John Dryden than Corneille; and as the next chapter will show, Dryden's dramatic theory and practice are steeped in Corneille, from whom he simultaneously tries to distinguish himself, in part by combining Corneille's dramatic form with the legacy of John Fletcher.

Tragicomedy to the Closure of the Theatres, September 1642

Given that so many of the outstanding successes in tragicomic form were collaborations, it is tempting to suggest that they lent themselves particularly to that form of composition. Since plot, character and discourse were manipulable in terms of mood and outcome, writers could exercise their particular talents in a single work. Almost like a relay race, a writer could get a piece off to a good start and then hand on the baton to a colleague particularly strong in the development phase. This is very much the feeling one derives from, for example, *The Spanish Gypsy* (1623), a play written by Ford, Dekker, Rowley and Middleton. Comprising four storylines, two of them derived from Cervantes' collection of stories the *Novelas Ejemplares*, each one involving a 'prodigal son' who has to rediscover his father, the play lends itself to a collaboration in which the participating authors do what each does best. It usefully summarizes many of the romance and tragicomic features that this chapter has witnessed in development. There is a pattern of sin, penitence and forgiveness expressed in a desire to turn back the clock. We hear tell of a daughter lost at sea who is to be revealed as the supernaturally beautiful and virtuous gypsy Preciosa. Spectators accustomed to tragicomedy know by now that, if there is a lost daughter, she will eventually turn up, probably in another identity. A band of gypsies provide this play's distinctive tonality – an inset play providing the music and dancing that dominates Acts 3 and 4 – and whose king is a nobleman needing to disguise himself.

Metatheatrical elements abound, commented upon by the characters themselves: 'Our comedy turned tragical!' (4.3.186). Political resonances with contemporary events are apparent. The story told in the most elevated rhetoric is that of Clara's abduction and rape at the hands of Roderigo, whom she eventually forgives and marries. Here, life imitated art. Set in Madrid, the play does not directly comment upon, but certainly resonates with the political events of 1623, a year in which Prince Charles's attempts to woo the Spanish Infanta had her fleeing him and crying rape when he jumped over the wall of the Casa del Campo to avoid protocols that kept them apart. *The Spanish Gypsy* performs its tragicomic function of generational repair and its trick of mingling high-born and low-born characters while ensuring that decorum is preserved by disguise and restoration of true aristocratic identity. Preciosa is not revealed to be noble before she can utter sentiments such as these:

> O, do not think, my lords, compassion thrown
> On a base, low estate, on humble people,
> Less meritorious than if you had favoured
> The faults of great men. (Middleton 2007: 1761; 5.1.115–18)

Since Guarini, as we have seen, tragicomedy in its pastoral, satirical and romantic variants has usually found space to express equalizing sentiments, even if more accommodating than radical in their depth of cut.

The continuing popularity of tragicomedy up to the 1642 theatre closure is demonstrated by the extent to which it features in the *oeuvres* of major playwrights in the Caroline period. James Shirley, who was writing between 1625 and 1642, wrote thirty-one plays, ten of which were classified as tragicomedies by the end of the seventeenth century. In 1653, a group of six was published by Humphry Robinson and Humphry Moseley, three of which, *The Doubtfull Heir*, *The Imposture* and *The Court Secret* – the latter having been prevented from performance by the theatre closure – are designated 'tragi-comedies' on their title pages. One further play, *The Gentleman of Venice*, is also so labelled. But, as stated, Shirley wrote several other tragicomedies, which are a major component of his successful career. John Ford's solo dramatic career begins and ends with tragicomedy, plays such as *The Lovers Melancholy* (1628) and *The Ladies Triall* (1638) establishing his credentials in the form.

Despite the deployment of pastoral to articulate social critique and anti-court sentiment, tragicomedy was, from the acquisition of the indoor Blackfriars playhouse by Shakespeare's King's Men in 1608, a form associated with the more socially exalted private theatres. Major editions of the Beaumont and Fletcher canon were published in 1647 and in 1679. Those editions, published in the republican period and after the Restoration, might have been explicitly preserving the culture of the Royalist regime, therefore. Plot complexity, use of spectacle, music and dance and, in Shakespeare's hands, classical mythology, the high-aspiring rhetoric of the serious parts of the storyline, metatheatricality making for in-crowd knowingness – such elements ensured that tragicomedy up to the 1642 theatre closure was not popular fare. Shirley and Ford, though not gentleman-amateur playwrights, were both from university backgrounds. Ford came from a well-to-do family and was trained in the Middle Temple. Both were connected to aristocratic patronage circles. Michael Neill's *ODNB* article on Ford emphasizes the extent to which he reworks earlier material, often Shakespearean (he appears to have had an obsession with *Othello*, a play to which he often returns), but subjects it to disorientating generic dislocations.[1] Audiences seldom know exactly where they are with Ford; and if tragicomedy as a genre has a tendency to wrongfoot its audiences with surprising turns of event, Ford's examples are in a class of their own. Susan Wiseman, editing a tragicomedy entitled *The Nice Valour* first printed in 1647 as part of the Beaumont and Fletcher canon but now credited to Middleton, points out that, by then, tragicomedy was considered to be a Royalist form, in contrast to city-based plays usually favoured by Middleton himself:

> *The Famous Tragedy of Charles I* (1649) includes a 'Prologue to the Gentry' which invokes the names of 'Jonson, Shakespeare, Goffe, and Davenant,/Brave Suckling, Beaumont, Fletcher, Shirley' claiming that they are 'loathed, by the Monsters of the times'. (Middleton 2007: 1679)

Tragicomedy was part of the 'Royalist claim to cultural capital' and therefore on the right side for the Restoration of 1660.

3

Restoration and Fall: Tragicomedy Restored

Meanwhile in Europe ...

In January 1637, Pierre Corneille's play *Le Cid* was premiered at the Marais theatre in Paris. Based on an earlier play *Las mocedades del Cid* (published in 1618 but possibly performed as early as 1599) by the Spanish dramatist Guillén de Castro (1569–1631), Corneille's version greatly simplifies his source play. He discards much of its baroque third act, to focus on a single incident in the life of Rodrigo Díaz de Vivar (*c.*1043–99), a Castilian knight given the honorific title El Cid deriving from the Arabic word for Lord. This incident is Rodrigo's revenge killing of his beloved Chimène's father, who has mortally insulted Rodrigo's own father. In historical fact, Rodrigo was appointed *armiger regis* or commander of the royal troops by King Sancho II of Castile, an appointment he lost to a rival nobleman, Count García Ordóñez, when Sancho was succeeded by his enemy Alfonso VI. This initiated a feud between the two noblemen that eventually resulted in military combat. In July 1074, probably at Alfonso's instigation, he married the king's niece Jimena, daughter of the count of Oviedo. The historical Cid does not appear to have murdered his betrothed's father; neither was he the Christian hero that de Castro and later Corneille represented him to be, though Corneille seems to have believed in the *Cid* he presented. He defended its veracity in an advertisement placed before the play in the 1648 edition of his works, citing Spanish sources for the story; and as late as 1660 he was still doing so. The Cid

LE CID

TRAGI-COMEDIE.

Ex libris Recollectorum conventus Pa

CVRVATA RESVRGO

A PARIS,
Chez AVGVSTIN COVRBE, Imprimeur & Libraire de Monſeigneur frere du Roy, dans la petite Salle du Palais, à la Palme.

M. DC. XXXVII.
AVEC PRIVILEGE DV ROY.

Figure 7 *Title-page of the 1637 first edition of Pierre Corneille's* Le Cid. *Photo by Culture Club/Getty Images.*

he inherited, however, was already a figure who was composed of history and legend in equal measure (Figure 7).

Corneille had tried his hand unsuccessfully at tragicomedy in 1630–1, with a play called *Clitandre.* Between that and *Le Cid*, he had won and lost the patronage of Richelieu and had retreated to his native Rouen to write. Much hinged on the success of *Le Cid* – and triumphant success it was. The form itself was nothing new – in Paris, some fifteen tragicomedies were performed in the years 1635–7 alone. *Le Cid*, however, was something altogether different. The tragicomic turn, the rescue from tragic destiny, was effected by having the heroine, Chimène, marry her lover Don Rodrigue, a happy enough resolution if it were not for the awkward fact that he has killed Chimène's father Don Gomès in a duel. Inflamed by jealousy over the appointment of Rodrigue's father Don Diègue as tutor to the royal princes, a position to which Gomès feels entitled by his military prowess and service to the state, the Count Gomès has slapped the venerable Diègue's face, an unpardonable insult that he is too old to revenge in person, so the duty falls to his son. Chimène's honour can only be satisfied by Rodrigue's death. Rodrigue is willing to die, but only at her hands. She, though, wishes for public justice, not to be her lover's private executioner. Chimène would be no dutiful daughter if she did not demand the death of her father's killer; and if she were not a dutiful daughter, she would be unworthy of Rodrigue. Rodrigue would be no man of honour if he did not avenge his father; and if he were not a man of honour, he would be unworthy of Chimène. Thus, the play is symmetrically balanced at the close of Act 3, with the added complication that the Infanta, the King of Castille's daughter, also loves Rodrigue but his relatively low social rank renders him unworthy of her – and anyway he loves Chimène.

A personal love-versus-honour dilemma goes public when Rodrigue leads a band of followers to repel an attack from the Moors. So valiantly does he perform that he gains the honorific title 'Le Cid' (Lord) from the Moors themselves. As Chimène petitions Don Fernand, King of Castille for justice, the King perceives the defendant as the saviour of the state whose father has after all suffered the most shameful insult. As is the situation in Shakespeare's *Coriolanus*, the King is doubtful whether the state can survive at all without its nuclear weapon Rodrigue. Don Fernand is understandably anxious to break the impasse, but where is a solution to be found? Fernand invokes an ancient law whereby he invites champions to combat Rodrigue, with Chimène's hand as the reward. Master of realpolitik, he adds the proviso that she will wed Rodrigue if the latter is victorious. Don Sanche takes up the challenge. Here, the tragicomic meme of apparent death and resurrection is twice deployed. First, the King pretends that Rodrigue has been killed in the combat against the Moors, eliciting a reaction from Chimène that proves she loves him. Then, Don Sanche enters to report that he has lost the duel with Rodrigue but that the latter has shown him clemency. Seeing him alive, however, Chimène assumes Rodrigue is dead. His 'resurrection' is the mechanism that enables Chimène to accept the pragmatic course of marrying the man she loves, the man above all men whom she should not wed. Audiences might perceive some weakening of her principle in this final peripeteia. The hapless Don Sanche is repellent to her – avoiding him looms just a little larger than it should, given that she has agreed to the terms. This suggestion that her honour may be a posture, a role played well in the face of perceived societal expectations, is inherited by Corneille from Guillén de Castro's original.

In Corneille's spare, concentrated Alexandrine rhyming couplets, this play has an effect that no English tragicomedy had attempted to create. Because both duels and the battle against the Moors are all reported actions that do not happen onstage, the play has a concentrated effect that derives from its appearing to observe the unities of time, place and action. French dramatists and critics were prepossessed with the idea that there were rules, prescribed by Aristotle, to which writers should adhere, the so-called 'unities'. (In English playwriting, this was a factor that had separated Ben Jonson's practice from Shakespeare's; and in post-1660 critical discussion, the topic is given considerable salience.) By the severe standards of the Académie Française, the judgement would be that Corneille had not complied. Focusing on debate rather than action – on what the characters have to say as they struggle to reconcile high principles of honour and duty with intense emotional pressures of love and loathing – produces a claustrophobic superheat. No farcical or comic action detracts from the verbal confrontations that constitute the play. It becomes a boiling cauldron in which Rodrigue and Chimène think out the imperatives that gendered conceptions of honour and duty impose upon them. There is a move-countermove chess-match rhythm to the dialogue, represented by stichomythia – alternating single lines of speech, often, but not in this case, witty. Resurrection is a key meme as we have seen, but few other memes operating in English tragicomedy are deployed. The two duennas, Léonor the governess to the Infanta and Elvire, governess to Chimène, do act as protector figures. Both labour to soften the edges of their mistresses' honour codes, helping the audience to feel that a compromise might conceivably be reached. *Le Cid* is not, however, a tragicomedy by virtue of working in a mixed mode, with blended scenes. By comparison to English tragicomedy, Corneille's is an intellectual form, nobility of expression being its ultimate value. Its unremitting relevance makes for a purity of purpose entirely different from the English practice.

When he was refused a supplementary payment of one hundred *livres* after the play's success, Corneille took out the publication rights and published a poem, 'Excuse à Ariste', protesting the originality and independence of the play, sparking off what came to be known as the 'querelle du Cid'. Jealous rival playwrights Scudéry and Mairet wrote against Corneille. Scudéry in his *Observations sur le* Cid (1637) was incensed that Corneille could permit Chimène to marry her father's murderer. Richelieu was persuaded to set up an investigating committee of the Académie Française, on whose behalf Jean Chapelain (1595–1674) reported on 20 December 1637 in his *Les Sentimens de l'Académie Française sur la tragicomédie du Cid*:

> l'auteur du *Cid* a failli, qui, trouvant dans l'histoire d'Espagne que cette fille avait épousé le meurtrier de son père, devait considérer que ce n'était pas un sujet de poème accompli parce qu'étant historique, et par conséquent *vrai, mais non vraisemblable.*
>
> (the author of the *Cid* is a failure [moral bankrupt], who, finding in Spanish history that this girl married her father's murderer, should have considered that this was not a suitable subject for a successful drama because [even if] it was historical and therefore *true,* [it] was not *plausible.*)[1]

A 'poème epique ou dramatique' must offer pleasure, but it must be 'un plaisir utile' (a 'useful pleasure' [Chapelain 1638: 34]). This aim will not be achieved if the play is not 'vray-semblable'. Several factors sabotage verisimilitude: a 'mauvais sujet' ('bad subject': 29–30); but the most crucial factor is that 'il y faut garder la biensceance' ('it must preserve decorum': 35). The poem or play must adhere to the 'moeurs' ('customs') of the time. Corneille's Chimène does not comply with 'biensceance de moeurs' ('decorum of manners') and therefore her behaviour is not useful for listener or audience (36). There are truths which should be suppressed for the public good (38), and the action must be altered if it does not conform to the customs of the time (39). The dénouement is deemed 'mauvais et contre l'art' ('wicked and opposed to art': 112). Chapelain offers this summary of why the play is so unsatisfactory: 'Le poete voulant que ce Poeme finist heureusement, pour suivre les regles de la Tragi-comedie' ('the dramatist wants the poem to end happily in order to follow the rules of tragicomedy': 121). Chapelain upheld Scudéry's point: not everything that has actually happened is suitable for theatrical representation. Drawing a distinction between *la vraisemblance* (that which is plausible) and *la verité* (that which is true, or has happened), he insisted on the importance of *les bienséances* (the proprieties) in theatrical representation. The proper thus becomes a compromise between the plausible and the true. Jean Chapelain was to uphold the case made by Corneille's rivals, even to the extent of suggesting how he could have ended the play: the Count could have turned out not to be Chimène's real father, or could have recovered from his injuries. Certainly this would have made even more use of the 'resurrection' meme!

Lying behind the debate is the Aristotelian question of mimesis: how is the imitation of reality to be most plausibly carried out? Implausibility is created by breaching the unities, thought the scholars of the Académie. If an action lasts longer than twenty-four hours, if it deals with a plethora of characters and events, if it moves about restlessly from one place to another: in all those cases, plausibility is ruptured. Implausibility also results from representing actions that are so far out of the common run of human affairs that they will induce in the spectator a sense of self-consciousness, a heightened awareness of theatrical illusion. When in Euripides' *Medea* a mother kills her own children, for example, even if in history such things have happened, this is an act contrary to nature and in the opinion of the Academicians is an affront to reason. Representing a marriage between a woman and the murderer of her father creates shock and surprise that shows the hand of the author behind the spectacle. Paradoxically, the result of representing real events can be a heightened awareness of artifice. This is a fascinating argument, perhaps not as absurd as it seems. The questions posed by the evolution of what comes to be known as neoclassical aesthetics are not as arid as they are sometimes considered to be. Indeed, they have never altogether disappeared. I once had occasion to ask the novelist David Lodge what he did about coincidences in his novels. He replied that several coincidences that had actually happened to him, he would not put in his novels because they would simply sound creaky and would not be believed. The rationing of coincidences in the interests of plausibility is a descendant of the neoclassical discussion around *vraisemblance*. The debates initiated by the 'querelle du Cid' would resonate much later in English thinking about tragicomedy when the theatres reopened after the Restoration.

The Cid was of great interest to English spectators and readers, no doubt because of the trouble it caused in France. Corneille's play was very soon available in English, translated by Joseph Rutter, a playwright with a special interest in tragicomedy. His *The Shepheard's Holy-day: a pastorall tragicomaedie* had been acted at Whitehall in 1633 and published in 1635, with commendatory verses supplied by no less a dramatist than Ben Jonson. His translation of *Le Cid* was acted in 1637 'before their Majesties at Court, and on the *Cock-pit* Stage in *Drury*-lane, by the servants to both their MAJESTIES'. Rutter was tutor to the 4th Earl of Dorset's sons, and he does not lose the opportunity to tell us, in the printed edition dedicated to Dorset, that the translation was done at Dorset's behest: 'I no sooner was commanded to translate this Poem by you than I went about it' (second edition, 1650: A2r); nor to compare Dorset's life somewhat improbably with that of the historical Cid. Rutter's blank verse translation rejects Corneille's occasional use of soliloquy, which he considers '*little pertinent to the business*' and makes some small changes to the play's opening; otherwise, it is faithful though it does lack the grandiloquence of the original. Interestingly, Rutter thinks Corneille's play is '*a true History, though like a Romance*' (A4r), and proposes it as a model for English writers.

English Tragicomedy Resumes

In 1665–6, as the plague raged in England, Isaac Newton was exiled from Cambridge to his remote Lincolnshire birthplace of Woolsthorpe, where he kept himself busy with integral and differential calculus, optics and gravity. Newton described his *annus mirabilis* in a later biographical memoir that provides a backdrop for a rational, scientific age – an age in which it can seem that literature is just as rule-governed as Newton discovered physics to be. John Dryden, the Restoration's principal tragicomedian, was to wrestle with the prescriptions of inflexible French criticism throughout his career. He spent some of *his* plague year in retirement writing an essay *Of Dramatick Poesy* (1668) that is considered by many to be the finest essay on theatre of its era. Tragicomedy is for Dryden a major concern. Cast in the form of a discussion conducted through a series of set speeches made by four speakers called Eugenius, Crites, Lisideius and Neander, representing prominent aristocratic literati then actively participating in the intellectual life of King Charles II's court (respectively Charles Lord Buckhurst, Sir Robert Howard, Sir Charles Sedley and Dryden himself), the essay discusses the state of modern theatre. There is a suggestion that the name 'Lisideius' is a play on *Le Cid*, both appropriate and ironic because Lisideius, though he is a stout defender of French theatre, is also an opponent of tragicomedy. His objection is stated thus:

> There is no theatre in the world has any thing so absurd as the English tragi-comedy; 'tis a drama of our own invention ... here a course of mirth, there another of sadness and passion, a third of honour, and fourth a duel: thus, in two hours and a half we run through all the fits of Bedlam. (Watson 1971: 1.45)

Covert ironies of many kinds operate here. Lisideius does not appear to know that Corneille called *Le Cid* a tragicomedy and thought of it as such. Does he know that his description of absurd English tragicomedy is a good fit for Dryden's *The Rival Ladies*, performed in 1664 and proudly announced as a 'tragi-comedy' on its title page? He appears to be echoing sentiments voiced by one of Dryden's rivals, Sir Robert Howard, who, in a preface 'To the Reader' that appears before his 1665 collection of *Four New Plays*, says this:

> our best Poets have differed from other Nations ... in usually mingling and interweaving Mirth and Sadness through the whole Course of their Plays ... and I confess I am now convinc'd in my own Judgment, That it is most

> proper to keep the Audience in one entire disposition both of Concern and Attention; for when Scenes of so different Natures immediately succeed one another, 'tis probable the Audience may not so suddenly recollect themselves, as to start into an enjoyment of the Mirth, or into a concern for the Sadness; Yet I dispute not but the variety of this World may afford pursuing Accidents of such different Natures; but yet though possible in themselves to be, they may not be so proper to be Presented. (Howard 1665: A4v, italics reversed)

The final sentence echoes the findings of the French Academy on *vraisemblance*. It must have been particularly hurtful to Dryden because Howard had collaborated with him over a play, *The Indian Queen* (1664), that is a tragicomedy in all but name, published by Howard as one of his four new plays. Unsurprising, therefore, that he should represent Howard as the snippy, captious Crites in the essay.

Neander, generally considered to be Dryden's own mouthpiece, then weighs in. He begins by pointing out that all the major French dramatists including Molière, Quinault and Corneille have been writing tragicomedies recently. He is careful to praise the English way of writing tragicomedy above the French (because after all one tendency of *Of Dramatick Poesy* is nationalistic and patriotic), but he argues that in principle following a 'scene of great passion' with one 'of mirth and humour' is not problematic because there is no reason to think 'the soul of man more heavy than his senses'. This is a similar argument to those with which slavish attention to the unities was combatted in English theoretical writing: 'it's the imagination, stupid'. We are endowed with the powers of imagination, so that if a playwright wishes to stage a scene inside the hull of a sailing ship, as Dryden does in *Rival Ladies*, why not? Similarly, he sees no objection to blended stagecraft. This is his sonorous conclusion:

> I must therefore have stronger arguments ere I am convinced that compassion and mirth in the same subject destroy each

> other; and in the mean time cannot but conclude, to the honour of our nation, that we have invented, increased, and perfected a more pleasant way of writing for the stage than was ever known to the ancients or moderns of any nation, which is tragi-comedy. (Dryden 1971: 1.58)

In one respect, though, Neander/Dryden is powerfully influenced by French practice and is prepared to defend it: writing in rhyming verse. Dryden was deeply influenced by the dignified nobility of Corneille's rhyming hexameters in *Le Cid*. *Of Dramatick Poesy* is steeped in the theoretical writings of Corneille, many times citing passages from his various *Examens* and *Discours*. In the first two stanzas of the Prologue to his 1667 tragicomedy *Secret Love*, Dryden pays homage to his major influences:

> He who writ this, not without pains and thought,
> From *French* and *English* Theaters has brought
> Th' exactest Rules by which a *Play* is wrought.
>
> The Unities of Action, Place, and Time;
> The Scenes unbroken; and a mingled chime
> Of *Johnson*'s humour, with *Corneille*'s Rhyme.
> (ll. 1–6, italics reversed)

Dryden sees himself as combining the best aspects of Ben Jonson's comedy with the dignity of Corneille's rhyme, creating an Anglo-French dramatic concordat. Dryden combats the contention of Crites/Howard that rhyme is not natural speech and therefore dialogue written in rhyme cannot be properly called imitation of life (mimesis). Serious plays represent 'nature', argues Neander, 'but 'tis nature wrought up to an higher pitch. The plot, the characters, the wit, the passions, the descriptions, are all exalted above the level of common converse, as high as the imagination of the poet can carry them with proportion to verisimility' (Dryden 1971: 1.87). Although he does not argue specifically for rhyme to be deployed in tragicomedy in *Of Dramatick Poesy*, confining himself to 'serious' plays, he does do so in the dedication to Roger, Earl of Orrery prefixed to *The Rival Ladies*.

Dryden's Tragicomedy

Audiences for Dryden's first tragicomedy *The Rival Ladies* (1664) might have been more interested in female form than in tragicomic form. The play deploys the Restoration's greatest theatrical discovery, the actress, to provocative effect. Two young beauties, Honoria and Angellina, are both in love with the same man, Don Gonsalvo. They disguise themselves as boys, respectively Hippolito and Amideo, affording the audience much gender-based pleasure as sexual rivalry forces the cross-dressed women to step up to the masculine plate and fight a duel. The timidity of women put in such a position had been a source of comic laughter since Viola's mutually terrified duel with Sir Andrew Aguecheek in *Twelfth Night*. Having access to female bodies, Dryden deploys both homoerotic and heteroerotic sexuality to the limits of decorum. As the two women unbutton, Amideo notices something:

> How's this!
> Two swelling Breasts! a Woman, and my Rival! (Dryden 1664: 47)

Seconds later, when Amideo '*Tears open his Doublet*', Hippolito makes the same discovery. Pepys found it to be 'a very innocent and most pretty witty play' (4 August 1664). His notion of innocence might require further investigation!

As far as tragicomedy is concerned, the play sets about reconciling recent French and earlier English achievement in the form. This is a case of striking a balance between English 'humour' and French 'exaltation', between the static, verbal nature of French tragicomedy and the rumbustious all-action English heritage. The erotic material we might perceive as part of the play's English humour. More Frenchified is the content that derives from the demands put upon love by honour, the key theme in *Le Cid* as we have seen. Don Gonsalvo and Don Rhodorigo (so called in the Personae Dramatis but usually called Rodorick in the play itself) are in love with the same woman, Julia, who is promised to Rodorick. The latter is represented throughout as an unpleasant curmudgeon in every way unworthy of Julia's love – even *he* remarks upon how dislikeable he is, referring to his 'peevish Jealousies' and his 'sullen Humour', and calling himself 'froward' (p. 68) – but Julia is honour bound to marry him. She has, however, been given to Gonsalvo by her brother Don Manuel. In a lengthy passage conducted in rhyming pentameters, Julia pleads with Gonsalvo to release his hold on her and leave her free to love Rodorick, the whole sequence performed kneeling:

> **Jul.** *You have the Pow'r to make my Happiness*
> *By giving that which you can ne'er possess.*
>
> **Gons.** *Give you to* Rodorick? *there wanted yet*
> *That Curse to make my Miseries compleat.*
>
> (42)

Dryden deploys rhyme for this long interview, though most of the rest of the play is in unrhymed blank verse, because here the characters are at their most overwrought. Here they are most 'exalted above the level of common converse' and, as Dryden argued in *Of Dramatick Poesy*, plausibly capable of speaking in 'spontaneous' rhyme. To arbitrate the respective claims of male and female conceptions of honour required rhyme, as Dryden perceived that it had in Corneille's *Le Cid*.

Memes commonly occurring in pre-Civil War tragicomedy are picked up by Dryden. We witness the device of the injured inamorata, as Gonsalvo, thrusting at Rodorick with his sword, '*hurts* Julia *in the Arm*' (34). Towards the play's close, Gonsalvo, whose nobility has required him to sacrifice his love for Julia to Rodorick, tries to persuade the latter to accept her hand. Rodorick replies charmlessly:

> Would'st thou make me the Tenant of thy Lust,
> To Toyl, and for my Labour take the Dreggs,
> The Juicy Vintage being left for thee?
> No; She's an Infamous, leud Prostitute;
> I loath her at my Soul.
>
> (52–3)

The men fight, Rodorick falls to Gonsalvo, makes a dying speech and swoons away. Readers of this book will not be surprised to learn of his later resurrection and availability to marry Julia – a device assisted by the fact that Don Rodorick is revealed to be Don Gonsalvo's long-lost brother. Neither will it surprise them that a would-be robber shown clemency by Gonsalvo in the play's opening scene is revealed at the end to be the Captain who puts in place the arrangements for the rescue of the principals from captivity by pirates – the 'protector' figure. Tragicomic memes come to the rescue.

The other developmental feature in *The Rival Ladies* is its use of masque. Masques, incantations and inset plays have usually been set in rhyme in earlier English tragicomedy, a metatheatrical linguistic marker suggesting that the language here is not the 'natural' language spoken by the characters. Dryden's masque is on the same theme that we perceived to operate in the deep structure of *Winter's Tale* – the myth of the rape of Persephone/Proserpine. Spectacular effects are introduced of a kind that, pre-Civil War, would only be staged in private theatres. Now, they are being brought to spectators in public venues. The stage directions are as follows:

> Towards the end of the Dance, *Rodorick* in the Habit of *Pluto*, rises from below in a black Chariot all Flaming, and drawn by black Horses; he Ravishes *Julia*, who personated *Proserpine*, and as he is Carrying her away, his Vizard falls off. *Hippolito* first discovers him.
>
> **Hip.** A Rape, A Rape; 'tis *Rodorick*, 'tis *Rodorick*.
>
> (34)

This play, then, offers audiences a distinctively new dramatic experience: French dignity set in English action; titillating eroticism amidst the spectacular effects of masque; rhyming couplets competing in the dialogue with blank verse – and familiar tragicomic memes structuring the overall dramatic trajectory.

Marriage à la Mode

One reason for the continuing popularity of tragicomedy into the 1670s (Dryden had written seven tragicomedies by 1671) is surely that the restoration to the throne of Charles II in 1660 *was* a kind of tragicomedy, to royalist eyes. As we have seen, tragicomedy as a form was closely associated with the previous royal culture, deliberately preserved in such publications as Moseley's editions of Beaumont and Fletcher. Tragicomedy is on the cultural level one means of effacing the gap between the 1630s and the Restoration. To the dark miseries of bloody civil war, regicide, the republic and the Protectorate, the restoration of the English monarchy, bringing in train the restoration of the Church of England, the House of Lords and the institution of theatre, could seem to be a happy ending. The mythologizing of Charles's escape after the Battle of Worcester in 1651, his shelter in the oak tree in Boscobel Wood, Shropshire, was an adventure story in itself that would not have been out of place as an incident in a tragicomic plot. This cultural memory of civil strife followed by glorious restoration is written into the DNA of Dryden's most artistically successful tragicomedy *Marriage à la Mode*. Set against a background of earlier civil war, the play's rightful prince Leonidas speaks of 'my right restored' (5.1.429), the parallel with Charles's restoration being difficult to miss. Oddly, Dryden presented the play as a comedy, not a tragicomedy, but by 1691 Langbaine was calling it a tragicomedy. The date of first performance is unknown but evidence points to late 1671.

Marriage à la Mode provides a clear illustration of what tragicomedy was becoming in Dryden's hands, how it was being redefined in terms of plot separation or 'double plot'.

The play contains two relatively separate actions – only 'relatively' because in fact the plots are interdependent at key moments and because they throw reflections on each other. The main or high plot is inhabited by exalted persons of elevated rank with some of the exposition being in verse. Upon this plot hinges the very future of the state, as the consequences of Polydamas's usurpation of the Sicilian throne are worked through. The rightful prince Leonidas and his beloved Palmyra have been brought up obscurely amongst fishermen. As the plot twists and turns, Leonidas is wrongly said to be Polydamas's son, and is subsequently demoted to commoner status when Palmyra is revealed as his daughter. All of this identity manipulation is effected through the benevolent deceptions practised by Leonidas's foster-father Hermogenes, who finally causes Leonidas to be recognized as the son of the true king and restored to the throne, while his beloved Palmyra proves to be Polydamas's daughter. Their love endures these sudden changes in status and the attendant alterations in the balance of power between them. Leonidas has to resist the advances of a powerful court lady, Amalthea, whose brother Argaleon is a corrupt favourite determined to have Palmyra and preserve the usurper Polydamas in power.

The second action involves four characters of lower (but not low) status, most of whose intrigues are conducted in prose. In this plot, Doralice who is married to Rhodophil, falls in lust with her husband's recently returned friend Palamede at first encounter. (The word used is 'love', but that seems a misnomer for what is actually a sexual adventure.) Palamede has returned home to marry Melantha, a Frenchified, affected lady who haunts the court, desperately avid for any sign of the princess Amalthea's favour. Rhodophil has Melantha in mind for a mistress. The ensuing action is summed up perfectly by Palamede:

> This is just thrust and parry with the same motion; I am to get his wife, and yet to guard my own mistress. But I am vilely suspicious that, while I conquer in the right wing, I shall be routed in the left; for both our women will certainly

> betray their party, because they are each of them for gaining of two. (Dryden 1978: 356; 3.2.130–5)

The military imagery deployed by Palamede here becomes a staple of Restoration sex plays. The thesaurus of views that comes to define the era's comedy and gains for it a bad reputation in subsequent critical reception is present in the secondary plot of Dryden's play: marriage is inherently boring and only the adventure of extramarital affairs can make it tolerable. Military, hunting and gastric imagery is deployed to metaphorize sexual relations. Rhodophil's speech to Palamede at 1.1.132–44 is a handy grab-bag of such attitudes. But *Marriage à la Mode* strays into uneasy territory when, after encounters in which the four unconvincingly if wittily preserve the pretence that their relationships are innocent and above board, Palamede makes this proposal:

> What dost think of a blessed community betwixt us four, for the solace of the women, and relief of the men? Methinks it would be a pleasant kind of life: wife and husband for the standing dish, and mistress and gallant for the dessert. (Dryden 1978: 383; 5.1.321–4)

Here the play's political unconscious coalesces with its libidinal economy. This suggestion of a commune revives memories of radical sects during the Civil War, some of whom advocated free love; the arrangement suggested is a kind of republic. There are problems with communal ownership, voiced by Rhodophil who says 'we had as good make a firm league not to invade each other's propriety [property]' (330). 'Propriety' keys us into a libidinal economy in which women are a circulating currency and the male investment is in banking as much of it as possible while denying it to the rival male. The couples are reconciled because, when each male perceives that his rival is attracted to his woman, her stock rises.

The high and low plots seem worlds apart. At times the clash of registers between the louche, queasy sexuality of the latter and the high-minded absoluteness of the former is so extreme as to challenge the possibility of coexistence. This seems a far cry from the Fletcherian conception of mixed mode as having low and high personages coexisting in a single action. Operatively, though, because both plots involve crossing vectors of love and desire, the parallels between them are easy to observe. They intersect directly when Melantha is attempting to attract the attention of court ladies and when, at the close, Leonidas asserts his right to the Sicilian throne by means of armed rebellion. Rhodophil and Palamede are career soldiers, the former Captain of the King's Guard, and the success of the rebellion depends upon their throwing in their lot to support Leonidas. In fact, the play's happy resolution is achieved by plot interdependence. Thematically, both plots explore the concept of honour: but whereas in the high plot honour is tied to a set of deep-rooted cultural assumptions about how high-born men and women ought to behave, in the low plot the term has dwindled into a word for female chastity, a commodity for which men and women can barter. In its main plot, *Marriage à la Mode* is steeped in, and shaped by, earlier tragicomedy.

Although the play has a possible source in seventeenth-century French prose romance, Madeleine de Scudéry's *Artamène: ou le Grand Cyrus* (in English translation 1653–5), readers of this book should need little persuasion that its more significant inspirations are *The Winter's Tale* and *Le Cid.* Plot resemblances with *Winter's Tale* are perceptible in the supernaturally beautiful couple being raised in obscure pastoral circumstances (compare Florizel and Perdita), who have been spirited away in babyhood by Hermogenes (Antigonus) with a companion, Eubulus, and with Polydamas's queen Eudoxia, apparently deceased but actually revealed by Eubulus to be living 'in a religious house' (compare Hermione). Eubulus returns towards the play's end as one of the Protector figures that recur in tragicomedy (compare Paulina). Like Leontes, Polydamas's tyrannical approach to rule renders him prone to pronouncing death sentences, so that the main plot is conducted in the shadow of the gallows. In 4.4, Palmyra and Leonidas have a dialogue conducted entirely in rhyming verse, in which Leonidas explains that he must press his title to the throne – that is the duty imposed upon him by his rank and gender. Palmyra's reply is exactly that of Chimène in *Le Cid*, though somewhat flatly expressed:

> And is it thus you court Palmyra's bed?
> Can she the murd'rer of her parent wed?
> Desist from force: so much you well may give
> To love, and me, to let my father live. (Dryden 1978: 371–2; 4.4.60–3)

She cannot marry the prospective murderer of her own father. Love-versus-honour marital dilemmas such as occur in the main plot, the postures that derive from fixed gender roles – 'Palmyra: Man's love may, like wild torrents overflow, / Woman's as deep, but in its banks must go' (4.4.46–7) – are ironically reflected in the shifting, liquid alliances of the secondary plot. Compare:

> **Rhodophil** There's something of antipathy in the word *marriage* to the nature of love; marriage is the mere ladle of affection, that cools it when 'tis never so fiercely boiling over.
>
> (4.1.164–6)

These views are a long way from one another. *Marriage à la Mode* is a play in constant tension with itself.

Why did Dryden not present his play as a tragicomedy, since the main plot describes a classic tragicomic parabola? Answers are speculative, but I think that Dryden had more invested in his comic secondary plot than in his somewhat routine main action. On matters of social status, *Marriage à la Mode* is an insecure play written by an insecure dramatist. Dryden was morbidly sensitive to his standing with the aristocracy, as his dedication to Rochester proves – a nobleman with whom he would soon be in open dispute. Witty exchanges between Doralice, Palamede and Rhodophil drive the comic plot in the direction of comedy of manners, a form that depends on an acute sense of social positioning, which this play makes explicit:

> **Doralice** [Y]our little courtier's wife, who speaks to the king but once a month, need but go to a town lady, and there she may vapour and cry 'The king and I' at every word. Your town lady, who is laughed at in the circle, takes her coach into the city, and there she's called Your Honour, and has a banquet from the merchant's wife, whom she laughs at for her kindness. And as for my finical cit, she removes but to her country house, and there insults over the country gentlewoman that never comes up, who treats her with frumity and custard, and opens her dear bottle of *mirabilis* beside, for a gill-glass of it at parting.
>
> (3.1.140–7)

Here is as clear a map of London snobbery *c.*1670 as can be found anywhere. The pecking order is court→town→city→country. 'Town' here stands for the socially improving, richer districts of the developing west end of London, inhabited by the gentility rather than the commerce-dominated tradespeople of the City of London. Melantha is a projection of such social anxiety. Each day she collects from her woman Philotis a list of new French words and expressions. Those she treats in a reified way, almost as actual *things*; indeed, she trades them with Philotis for her cast-off clothing. She is determined to introduce French loan words into her conversation, believing that her Francophile manners will bring her success at court. At one obvious level, Dryden is tilting at the Francophile complexion of the courtiers who returned from exile in France after 1660. I wonder, though, if he may also be satirizing the form of tragicomedy itself? Early in Act 5, Leonidas has been taken prisoner by the usurper Polydamas and is paraded over the stage under armed guard. This is the bizarre juncture that Melantha chooses to bother Palmyra with her catalogue of French words, only to find herself being unceremoniously snubbed. Palamede observes all this because he has been hoping to win Melantha with his own specious command of French vocabulary. In Act 5, Scene 1, a sequence is conducted in macaronic Franglais (ll. 112ff.) to which Philotis contributes, in which Melantha furiously blames Palamede for her discomfiture. She alternately cries and laughs, wheedled into good humour by snatches of song taken from Molière's recent play *Le Bourgeois Gentilhomme* (1670). The intersection between the two plots at this point seems so absurd, so *mal à propos* (to use one of Melantha's favourite expressions), that I read it more as a satire on tragicomic form itself than as one of the blended tragicomic scenes we have earlier encountered. Melantha's emotional barometer, moving from tears to laughter in an instant, may be a *reductio* of comic rabbits coming out of tragic hats that the main plot is busy bringing to pass. If my reading has any force, it suggests the commencement of tragicomedy's weakening hold over the playgoing public. The relative social realism of comedy of manners seems more appealing than the old hat, whether tragic or comic, offered by the stiff postures of duty and honour.

This is one lesson that Dryden was taught very shortly after *Marriage à la Mode* was first performed, when Buckingham's *The Rehearsal* was staged at the Theatre Royal, Drury Lane on 7 December 1671 – the same venue as Dryden's play. (As has been said, we don't know the date of Dryden's premiere, but parodies of *Marriage à la Mode* in *The Rehearsal* suggest that it was already available to audiences.) Bayes, a character whose resemblance to Dryden was emphasized in performance by the actor John Lacy, is taking us through a rehearsal of his new play for the benefit of two gentlemen called Smith and Johnson, which is so nonsensical that one cannot be sure of its genre (Figure 8). As the Prologue says:

For (changing Rules, of late, as if men writ
In spite of Reason, Nature, Art and Wit)
Our Poets make us laugh at Tragedy,
And with their Comedies they make us cry. (Villiers 1976: 11–14)

Figure 8 *John Graham's painting of Richard Suett playing Bayes in Buckingham's* Rehearsal *in 1796. Contemporary sources record that he had 'a most unpromising pair of legs'. Photo by The Print Collector/Getty Images.*

Parodies of Dryden's plays come thick and fast – not only Dryden's, but he is the principal target. A single example will suffice. In 3.4, Prince Pretty-man utters this absurd speech:

Bring in my Father; why d'ye keep him from me?
Altho a Fisherman, he is my Father,
Was ever Son, yet brought to this distress,
To be, for being a Son, made fatherless?
Ah, you just Gods, rob me not of a Father:
The being of a Son take from me rather.

(16–22)

Leonidas and Palmyra are brought up amongst fishermen. They are of 'uncommon beauty / And graceful carriage' (1.1.287–8), so Leonidas is a pretty man, as it were. Dryden's hopping up and down on lost and restored children, a standard tragicomic feature, is in the firing line here. The two-part *Conquest of Granada* (1670–1) is even more of a target than *Marriage*, but it too is a tragicomedy, a genre which looms larger than any other in the list of plays ridiculed. *The Rehearsal* is our first clear evidence that tragicomedy is losing its grip.

Improving Dryden

Dryden returned to tragicomedy a decade later, with a play called *The Spanish Fryar or, The double discovery* (1681, performed 1680). Perhaps significantly if mixed-mode drama is beginning to lose its box-office appeal, this is not presented as a tragicomedy on the title page – it is not labelled at all, simply given a title. In the remarkably self-congratulatory dedication to John, Lord Haughton, however, he speaks of 'the Care and Pains I have bestowed on this beyond my other Tragi-comedies' (A2r), efforts which in Dryden's opinion the present play has richly repaid. He must have concluded that *Marriage à la Mode* was compromised by the lack of integration between its two plots, because his conviction is that, in *The Spanish Fryar*, he has solved that problem. He points out that there are two 'Actions' in it and, as he says, either of them could have made a complete play. Audiences, though, are finding tragedies boring, says Dryden, 'for the Feast is too dull and solemn without the Fiddles' (A4v). Tragicomedies are not easy to write, however:

> Neither is it so trivial an undertaking, to make a Tragedy end happily; for 'tis more difficult to save than 'tis to kill. The Dagger and the Cup of Poison are alwaies in a readiness; but to bring the Action to the last extremity, and then by probable means to recover all, will require the Art and Judgment of a Writer; and cost him many a pang in the performance.
>
> (A4v–r)

At this point, we might pause to reflect on twists and turns. Fletcherian tragicomedy has always made plot a feature. Audiences did not seem to regard complex and at times unconvincingly coincidental plots as collateral damage attendant on fusing mixed actions, but as a source of pleasure in their own right. Suspense, largely ruled out by the inevitable throughline of tragedy, is an effect upon which tragicomedy can capitalize. Audiences are invited to be more interested in narrative than in character. In the passage quoted above, Dryden suggests that the writing, being in charge of twists and turns, is a skill in its own right. The plaintive voice of the professional writer addressing amateurs who might not understand how difficult this stuff is to do is clearly heard. Neglect of character, however, would eventually prove a fatal vulnerability.

Unlike *Marriage à la Mode*, where the play's involvement in politics is a cultural memory of the previous generation's civil war, *The Spanish Fryar* directly participates in the hate politics of its period. In the so-called 'Popish plot' of 1678, two mavericks called Titus Oates and Israel Tonge managed for a while to convince the King that there was a Catholic-inspired plot to poison him, contriving to have some twenty-two Jesuits executed and five Catholic peers put on trial. Subsequent attempts to exclude the King's brother James from the throne on the grounds that he was a Catholic (the 'Exclusion crisis') ensured that anti-Catholic feeling was running as high in 1680–1 as it ever has in British history. Loathing of the Jesuits and of Catholic religious orders was vitriolic. Dryden's play exploits this structure of feeling, tapping directly into it with his portrait of a Dominican friar, conveniently called Father Dominic, whose Falstaffian personality is a puffball of corruption. Father Dominic is a bibulous, venereal, bribe-taking monstrosity, only outdone in corruption by the character of Gomez, whose name declares that he is a Sephardic Jew.

Sir Walter Scott in his 1808 edition of Dryden's *Works* supports Dryden's claim to have successfully sutured the two actions together. To Scott, the main plot's language is more vivid, poetic and effective than that of any other tragicomedy Dryden wrote, but he has considerable difficulty with characterization. The Queen in the tragic, or main, plot consents to the murder of her consort, an aged and virtuous legitimate monarch, permitting her betrothed but despised Bertran to perform it so that she can later denounce him and marry Torrismond. In the event, the resurrection meme prevents this from happening – the King is not killed – and the restoration meme locates Torrismond's identity as the true king's son. To Scott, the Queen's conduct does not add up:

> The subsequent progress of the plot is liable to a capital objection, from the facility with which the queen, amiable and virtuous, as we are bound to suppose her, consents to the murder of the old dethroned monarch. We question if the operation of any motive, however powerful, could have been pleaded with propriety, in apology for a breach of theatrical decorum, so gross, and so unnatural. (Scott 1808: Works 6.370–1)

What Scott is objecting to is what we might now call the character's 'psychology'. He is putting his finger on what is to be perceived as a crippling weakness in the form. In Dryden's hands, tragicomedy has a stereotypical main plot representing high politics and affairs of state, staging love and honour conflicts between royal, military and aristocratic characters that are resolved by implausible and contrived turns of fortune. The real energy lies in the comic secondary plot. *The Spanish Fryar* owed its continuing popularity to its symbolic significance as Protestant propaganda. It was the only play forbidden by King James II; and when Queen Mary, James's daughter, came to the throne in 1689 after the so-called 'Glorious Revolution' brought over the Dutch House of Orange to rule England, it was the first play she asked for. As Scott remarked, that was 'a choice, of which she had abundant reason to repent, as the serious part of the piece gave as much scope for malicious application against herself, as the comic against the religion of her father' (371). There were many who regarded Mary II as an usurping queen married to a foreign invader. Ironically also, by 1685 Dryden had converted to Catholicism and was that religion's most significant laureate.

Improving Shakespeare

From an early Restoration version of Shakespeare and Fletcher's *The Two Noble Kinsmen* (performed 1613, first published 1634), the direction of travel in period adaptation of Shakespeare is already apparent. Davenant's adaptation, called *The Rivals*, was performed in 1664 and published in 1668. His main objective was domestication. He removed all the elements of ritual, mythology and medievalism from the original play, stripping out most of the material that modern editors give to Shakespeare and permitting much of the Fletcher to remain. Where the original ending has Arcite die a sacrificial death, blessing his rival Palemon's union with Emilia, Davenant simplifies this awkward triangular geometry, contriving a purely symmetrical and comic coming together of two couples. Much is done to raise the tone of the original, most obviously the elevation of the gaoler and his daughter in social rank, to the Provost and Celania. *The Rivals* does not make the demands on an audience required by late Shakespearean tragicomedy.

One way forward with Shakespeare was to rewrite tragedy as tragicomedy. A celebrated case of Shakespeare adaptation is the 'happy ending' version of *King Lear* made by Nahum Tate in 1681, a version that has been a joke, at least in academic circles, for centuries. Tate's version, though, held the stage until 1838, in further adaptations by George Colman (1768), David Garrick (1773) and John Philip Kemble, so he had the laugh for quite a lot of the time. What Tate did, readers of this book can see clearly, is superimpose on Shakespeare's tragedy the tragicomic pattern currently holding the stage. Tate's dedication to Thomas Boteler expresses what was to be a standard view of Shakespeare in the period: 'I found the whole ... a Heap of Jewels, unstrung and unpolisht; yet so dazzling in their Disorder, that I soon perceiv'd I had seiz'd a Treasure.' 'Polishing' importantly involved creating symmetrical pairs of characters. Neoclassical adaptors were obsessed with symmetry, going to absurd lengths to tie loose ends. Canons of symmetry and *vraisemblance* required that Edgar and Cordelia should be lovers; and having hit upon that idea, Tate was thrown upon 'making the Tale conclude in a Success to the innocent distrest Persons. Otherwise I must have incumbred the Stage with dead Bodies, which Conduct makes many Tragedies conclude with unseasonable Jests.' His authority for this is Dryden, and he quotes the passage from the Preface to *The Spanish Fryar* that we cited in the section 'Improving Dryden', about how difficult it is to make tragedies end happily. Tate considered his version of *Lear* to be a tragicomedy in the Drydenesque manner, though it is probable that too much of Shakespeare's original remains visible through the holes in the superstructure.

In this late-seventeenth-century culture, audiences are invited to view differently, to take different sorts of pleasure. It is customary to see Tate as diminishing the play by shaping it to be symmetrical but for his audience he was powerfully increasing its pleasure and importance. Of the alterations Tate made, the most important is the romance between Edgar and Cordelia that, if it does not enable a happy ending, at least avoids the nihilism of Shakespeare's. There are vital excisions as well as expansions: the Fool is done away with, presumably because Tate did not understand the character's dramatic function and was embarrassed by all that folly and madness. Lear's madness is considerably toned down to suit the taste of a more rational era. A smaller alteration but surprisingly important is the excision of the King of France. No longer the French king's consort, Cordelia is free to love Edgar. More importantly, the play becomes entirely *English*. The rebellion that unseats the unholy trinity of Goneril, Regan and Edmund is now entirely native, not the result of a foreign invasion: 'The Peasants are all up in Mutiny' (41) and are being whipped into frenzy by the sightless Gloster (so spelt) and by Edgar. Tate's *Lear* performs the triumph of *legitimacy*, not solely as a question of family bloodline:

Glost.

Where is my Liege? Conduct me to his Knees to hail
His second Birth of Empire; my dear *Edgar*
Has, with himself, reveal'd the King's blest Restauration.
(66)

In Tate's hands, *King Lear* re-enacts the tragicomic episode of British history that begins in civil war and ends in the happy restoration of legitimate monarchy. The characters are awestricken at the final turn of events. Albany has 'a Tale t'unfold so full of Wonder / As cannot meet an easy Faith' (64). Edgar's 'wondrous Story' (66) follows Lear's expression of disbelief: 'Is't Possible? / Let the Spheres stop their Course, the Sun make Hault, / The Winds be husht, the Seas and Fountains Rest' (65). Tragicomedy's trademark emotional effect is fully evident here.

Some of Tate's events and textures are dictated to him by his absorption of tragicomedy. In Act 3, Cordelia has acquired a servant-companion, Arante – for which respectable lady in the 1680s could go roaming about the wild countryside unattended, and which tragicomic heroine ever does? (Figure 9). Two ruffians sent by Edmund to abduct Cordelia for his sexual gratification are interrupted by the sudden arrival of the disguised Edgar. He reveals his true identity, despairing that since Cordelia rejected him when in his glory as a nobleman, she will surely have even less interest in him

Figure 9 *Susannah Cibber playing Cordelia in Nahum Tate's version of* King Lear *in 1755. From a later painting by Pieter Van Bleek. Photo by DeAgostini/Getty Images.*

now: 'what Reception must Love's Language find / From these bare Limbs and Begger's humble Weeds?' (36). The typical tragicomic peripeteia occurs:

> Come to my Arms, thou dearest, best of Men,
> And take the kindest Vows that e'er were spoke
> By a protesting Maid ...
> These hallow'd Rags of Thine, and naked Vertue,
> These abject Tassels, these fantastick Shreds,
> (Ridiculous ev'n to the meanest Clown)
> To me are dearer than the richest Pomp
> Of purple Monarchs.
>
> (36)

Here, Tate is picking up the pastoral theme that has been a texture of tragicomedy since its earliest inception in Guarini and Fletcher. When Tate is at his most cod-Shakespearean, for example at the beginning of Act 4, set in 'a Grotto', a stage direction placing '*Edmund* and *Regan* amorously Seated, Listning to Musick', with obvious indebtedness to the discovery of Ferdinand and Miranda playing chess in *The Tempest* 5.1, the source of his 'improving' inspiration is tragicomedy. For playwrights and audiences in the 1670s, symmetry and decorum are the aesthetic expression of political legitimacy. In the Dryden/Davenant adaptation of *The Tempest* as *The Enchanted Island* (1670, performed 1667), this is taken as far as it can go. Two new characters are invented for one another: Dorinda, sister to Miranda who like her has never seen a man, and Hippolito who has never seen a woman. Caliban has a sister, Sycorax, and at the very end of the play, even Ariel gains a partner, the biblically named sprite Milcha with whom he dances a saraband.

Tate's play does not seem so ridiculous, I hope, when one understands how it is intended to function generically, but nevertheless there is a failure to take on the full complexity of the tragicomic legacy, even that of Fletcher. When in 1687 Tate produced an 'improved' version of Fletcher's *The Island Princess*, immediately recognized by Langbaine as a tragicomedy in 1688, his intention was obvious from the dedication to Henry Lord Walgrave, the Royal Comptroller: 'the design of my Authors [he attributed it to Beaumont and Fletcher] in this Poem, was to shew transcendent Vertue, Piety and Constancy'. We have seen that Fletcher had no such simple intention: rather he bedevilled his audience with ambiguous characters whose uncertain morality was recruited for the defence of Protestant Christianity. Tate's play not only removes the bawdy from the original, but also excises the complex relationship between colonialism and religious evangelism. His character Pymero is a vastly simplified version of Fletcher's Pinheiro. Nowhere is Tate's reductive instinct more obvious than when it turns out that Quisara is only testing Armusia's virtue when she demands his religious conversion. She has already decided to convert and is only waiting for Armusia to prove the constancy of his faith.

Tragicomedy Waxes and Wanes: *The Fatal Marriage*

At the end of his career as a dramatist, Dryden recanted his views on tragicomedy. In the treatise he wrote to preface his translation of Du Fresnoy's Latin poem *De arte graphica* (1668) entitled 'A Parallel of Poetry and Painting' (1695), he says this:

> The Gothic manner, and the barbarous ornaments which are to be avoided in a picture, are just the same with those in an ill-ordered play. For example, our English tragi-comedy must be confessed to be wholly Gothic, notwithstanding the success which it has found upon our theatre, and in the *Pastor Fido* of Guarini; even though Corisca and the Satyr contribute somewhat to the main action. Neither can I defend my *Spanish Friar*, as fond otherwise as I am of it, from this imputation: for though the comical parts

> are diverting, and the serious moving, yet they are of an unnatural mingle: for mirth and gravity destroy each other, and are no more to be allowed for decent than a gay widow laughing in a mourning habit. (Dryden 1971: 2.202)

'A gay widow laughing in a mourning habit': the question of how to write integrated tragicomedy returns to haunt Dryden, forcing the admission that the solution is not to be found in the double-plot construction. By 1695, he might have been particularly jaded with the form. The Williamite revolution of 1688–91 replicated the tragicomic politics of the Restoration, at least for those on the winning side, a category that excluded Dryden. James II's Second Declaration of Indulgence (May 1688) was interpreted as a Trojan horse for Catholic toleration, which precipitated open revolt against him. Events followed in rapid succession: James's flight and capture at Sheerness, followed by an invitation issued by English grandees to William of Orange to accept the throne, his landing in Torbay, the Declaration of Rights followed by the Coronation of William and Mary (April 1689), the Jacobite uprisings in Scotland and Ireland in the wake of William's legitimation and the far-from-bloodless pacification of those countries – this sequence of events meant that, once again in the 1690s, civil society was divided between winners and losers. Between 1689 and 1695, tragicomedy had something of an Indian summer. Nine plays were printed with 'tragi-comedy' on their title pages. Others were identified by Langbaine or have been so identified since. A group of four anonymous tragicomedies was printed in 1690, all of them Williamite Whig plays celebrating the events of the Revolution, despite two of them, *The Abdicated Prince* and *The Bloody Duke*, being set in 'Alba Regalis', medieval Hungary! The preface to *The Royal Voyage* informs us that 'the End of this Play is chiefly to expose the Perfidious, Base, Cowardly, Bloody Nature of the Irish, both in this and all past Ages' (Anon. 1690: unnumbered), justifying current savage anti-Catholic actions in Ireland with reference to the Cromwellian campaigns of an earlier age.

Dryden's weary abreaction to tragicomedy may be explicable through such contextualization, but there is other evidence that the tide was turning against the genre. No less an authority than John Milton, in the prefatory essay 'Of that Sort of Dramatic Poem which is called a Tragedy' that introduces *Samson Agonistes* (1671), writes of 'the poet's error of intermixing comic stuff with tragic sadness and gravity; or introducing trivial and vulgar persons, which by all judicious hath been counted absurd; and brought in without discretion, corruptly to gratify the people' (Milton 1968: 344). He was writing this at around the same time as *Marriage à la Mode* was being staged, at the height of the post-Restoration fashion for tragicomedy, assuming (for we do not know for certain) that *Samson* was written close to the date of its publication. Whereas Milton objects to the commercial motives behind tragicomic writing, a 1684 translation of the Abbé d'Aubignac's *The Whole Art of the Stage* (1657) makes the argument that French tragicomedies are not at all what Plautus had in mind when he described *Amphitruo* under that name and, in any case, the term is not commercially useful. It gives the game away and wrecks the possibility of suspense:

> this title alone may destroy all the beauty of a Play, which consisting particularly in the *Peripetia*, or return of Affairs, it may discover that too soon; since the most agreeable thing in a *Dramma* is, that out of many sad and Tragick appearances, the Event should at last be happy, against the Expectation of the whole Audience; but when once the word *Tragicomedy* is prefix'd, the Catastrophe is presently known, and the Audience the less concern'd with all the Incidents that trouble the designs of the chief Actors; so that all their *Pathetick* complaints do but weakly move the Spectator, who is prepossessed with an Opinion that all will end well; whereas if we were ignorant of the Event, we should tremble for them, and be likewise more delighted with the return of good Fortune that should deliver them. (Hédelin 1684: 145)

A play that usefully defines the limits of what tragicomedy was and could achieve in the later seventeenth century is Thomas Southerne's *The Fatal Marriage; or, the Innocent Adultery* (1694). Strictly speaking this play has no place in our story because it is not a tragicomedy. Presenting it simply as a 'play' on the title page, Southerne nevertheless speaks in the dedication of '*the tragical part of this Play*' (which he has borrowed from one of Aphra Behn's novels, *The History of the Nun; or The Fair Vow Breaker* [1689]), adding that '*I have given you a little taste of Comedy with it*', this being derived, though Southerne does not say so, from Boccaccio's *Decamerone* (Southerne 1988: vol. 2, 10). From that description, we would predict that the play will follow the Drydenesque formula for a double-plotted tragicomedy. Isabella and her child have been left destitute by the loss, seven years earlier, of her husband Biron, killed in the Turkish wars. Biron's father Count Baldwin, who blames her for the ruin of his son, shows her no charity. Reluctantly, she accepts a marriage proposal from Villeroy, who rescues her from penury. In the parallel action, a jealous husband Fernando has his daughter Victoria stolen away by her brother Fabian for the benefit of his friend Frederick, the former disguised as a friar. By the end of Act 3, the outcome is truly unpredictable.

By the beginning of Act 4, the subplot is entirely reconciled. In an unusually literal deployment of the resurrection meme, Fabian drugs his father and has him transported to the family tomb. Convinced that there has been a genuine miracle – that he has in fact returned from the dead – Fernando revises his attitude to his wife Julia and daughter Victoria, happily accepting Frederick as a son-in-law. This action provides much opportunity for sport with the Catholic doctrine of Purgatory as a place where the souls of sinners can purge their sins prior to entering Heaven. In *The Fatal Marriage*, though, the resurrection meme turns septic. Entirely dissimilar to its functioning in tragicomedy, it is not here a mechanism for reconciliation. In the second half of the play, Isabella's first husband Biron returns from the wars. It is discovered that he has written letters to his brother Carlos, who has concealed the fact that Biron is alive in order to inherit his fortune. Isabella's position, rendered bigamous, is untenable. She loses her sanity and commits suicide, while Biron is killed by Villeroy. Carlos has not appeared as a villain until the play's end. The audience could not have predicted that the action would move in such a darkly tragic direction. It is as if Southerne had heeded d'Aubignac's advice: by labelling *The Fatal Marriage* a 'play' on the title page, he has given nothing away about how the action might develop.

By and large, we do not have the information needed to determine how commercially successful seventeenth-century plays were. Sources of information include Pepys's diary, which ends on 31 May 1669, and the bills sent to Charles II for theatre attendance and court performances; but we possess records of only around 7 per cent of known and estimated performance nights for the whole of the late seventeenth century.[2] In the case of this play, however, there is a letter dated 22 March 1694 received by a member of the Windham family of Felbrigg:

> It is not only the best that author ever writt, but is generally admired for one of the greatest ornaments of the stage, and the most entertaining play has appeared upon it these 7 years ... I never saw Mrs. Barry [Isabella] act with so much passion as she does in it; I could not forbear being moved even to tears to see her act. Never was poet better rewarded or incouraged by the town; for besides an extraordinary full house, which brought him about 140l. 50 noblemen, among whom my lord Winchelsea was one, gave him guineas apiece, and the printer 36l. for his copy. (Southerne 1988: vol. 2, 5)

The Fatal Marriage was both an aesthetic and a commercial success, its effect deriving from the fact that it manipulates familiar tragicomic memes in ways that wholly wrong-foot spectators. And it turns its back on the rhetoric and postures of the heroic plays that have formed the main plots in tragicomedies. For this play is a domestic tragedy, its language borrowing adeptly from the domestic passages of Jacobean dramas. At the end of 2.2, for example, Isabella is left on-stage alone, and expresses herself in a way reminiscent of John Webster's *Duchess of Malfi* (1623), 4.2.216–27:

> The worst that can befall me, is to dye:
> When once it comes to that, it matters not
> Which way 'tis brought about: Whether I Starve,
> Or Hang, or Drown, the end is still the same.
>
> (2.2.85–8)

Pathos simply expressed; and it derives from the domestic situation of having to look after her child without means, while her father-in-law spurns her and her few remaining possessions are being sequestrated. This is a predicament that speaks to us today as much as it did in 1694, something that cannot be said for the situations of most tragicomic main-plot protagonists. The love of both men for Isabella is sincerely and powerfully articulated, while Isabella's mental breakdown is as convincingly rendered as any theatrical insanity in the drama of the seventeenth century.

The Demise of Tragicomedy

Why am I occupying space with a play that does not end happily and is not, therefore, a tragicomedy? I wish to argue that we can see in *The Fatal Marriage* the beginnings of tragicomedy's obsolescence, resulting from cultural shifts transcending the drama itself. Silent forces of change have been operating across the theoretical discussions and the plays we have been examining. In the debates surrounding *vraisemblance*, we have been witnessing a plausibility crisis for the epic and forms such as heroic tragedy that derive from it.

Nahum Tate's happy-ending *Lear* is in part a domestication of tragedy, a reduction of its bleakly apocalyptic Shakespearean finale to manageable proportions. In the period between the English Civil War and the mid-eighteenth century, commercial capitalism transformed pre-industrial Britain into a consumer society. As demand for printed materials rose, stimulated by the Civil War itself, and literacy rates rose in the decades following the Restoration, English society became capable of delivering standards of living that were considerably above subsistence for many sections of society. Books were amongst the possessions that these improving individuals wanted to consume; hence the growth of the book market. By the 1690s, when newspapers and periodicals had become a permanent part of the publishing scene, when women were entering the literary workplace as consumers and producers, when theatre was becoming big business and when arguments had begun to be made about 'wit' or imagination as a form of intellectual property, we can speak of the beginnings of a mass market for literary and theatrical goods.

All of this had a profound effect on what was being written. New generations of readers and spectators, deriving from different social provenances, wanted to read new kinds of story and see new kinds of theatre – not stories with remote, ramrod-stiff protagonists, but stories coloured by decorous humour and concerning the lives of individuals whose destinies might conceivably resemble their own. In the last decade of the seventeenth century and into the eighteenth, much imaginative writing was aspiring to a new condition of narrativity, privileging the telling of relevant, domestic and sometime contemporaneous stories. Theatre developed in tandem with the novel in this respect; tragic and comic plots began to resemble one another as the classical genres lost their distinctiveness. The new tragicomic mixture itself became more domestic and bourgeois in scope. Elsewhere, borrowing a term from the cultural historian Mikhail Bakhtin, I have written of 'novelization', referring to a cultural process that took place in post-1660 England, making for the mingling and mixing of different literary modes within and between all major genres of writing (Hammond and Regan 2006).

Imaginative writing across all genres in the early eighteenth century was making for a new kind of discursivity. There was by now an extensive literature on the growth of the book market and the exponential increase in the value of literary property in the latter decades of the seventeenth century, leading to at least the legal possibility of authors owning the rights to their own writings, enshrined in the 1709 Act for the Encouragement of Learning (8 Anne c. 21). We can chart the spread of literacy, the post-1688 politico-ecclesiastical consensus that created a stability and relative press freedom, expressed in the 1695 Licensing Act not being renewed, weakening therefore the stranglehold of censorship. All of this was beneficial to the book trade. There is a gradual domestication of the literary agenda that enabled men *and* women from ever-widening social provenances to join the categories 'writer' and 'reader'. Of importance in understanding such developments is Jürgen Habermas's highly influential account of the emergence of a 'bourgeois public sphere' in the later seventeenth century: a theory of the development of public opinion. Habermas's definition given in *The Structural Transformation of the Public Sphere* (1962, first English translation 1989) refers to 'private people, [who] come together to form a public ... [to] compel public authority to legitimate itself before public opinion' (Habermas 1989: 25–6). Habermas made the argument, subsequently to become controversial, that these spaces are not merely virtual. Actual physical spaces developed to give new forms of polite conversation a local habitation and a name – coffee-houses, clubs and societies prominent amongst them, wherein the opinions of citizens could be expressed free from the trammels of the state and the church. As the eighteenth century progressed, the theatre itself became such a space. (An example might be the Old Price Riots of September 1809, stage managed by the Westminster Radicals, that organized a confrontation between audience and management. When the new Covent Garden Theatre opened at higher prices, a contestation of cultural and class privilege ensued.) Common people came to understand that they had a stake in their own governance and in this new and unique realm of discursive sociability, they came together to discuss such matters. In an inclusive, socially equalized sphere of print and orality, men could discuss their concerns. And if this was mainly a male phenomenon, literary periodicals, plays and novels could set women thinking about them also. The privatization of domestic architecture in middle-class homes produced spaces such as 'closets', where women could enjoy the pleasures of those new forms.

All of this is most readily discernible in the rise of the periodical essay, in particular the *Tatlers* and *Spectators* masterminded by Addison and Steele. With their problem pages, readers' letters, opinion-forming 'leader' essays covering a vast range of discourses, prominently the new middle-status discourse of 'taste', they were moving the direction of travel towards problem-solving and opinion-forming. Some of this is reflected in writing for the theatre and its effect was to squeeze out the space hitherto occupied by tragicomedy. As the seventeenth century gives place to the eighteenth, 'pathetic' tragedies such as *The Fatal Marriage* and the 'she-tragedies' of Nicholas Rowe, *The Fair Penitent* (1702/3, which is his adaptation of Massinger and Field's *The Fatal Dowry* [1632]), *Jane Shore* (1714) and *Lady Jane Grey* (1715), absorb energy from tragicomedy. Their concentration on the domestic dilemmas of the protagonists – Jane Shore, like Southerne's Isabella, finds her most terrifying jeopardy in the privations of hunger and destitution – paves the way for tragedies such as George Lillo's *The London Merchant* (1731) in which it is at last conceded that tragedy can be made out of the fates of entirely ordinary people. We no longer require the literary 'apartheid' of the double-plotted tragicomedy because separation of august personages from the little people is not necessary. We're all somewhere in the (upper) middle and we're all to an extent theatrically interesting.

Commencing around 1691 and reaching a climax with Colley Cibber's *Love's Last Shift, or, the Fool in Fashion*

(1696), a series of plays was written in which the subject of marital disharmony was explored more seriously than it ever had been before. The postures of older sex comedy, such as held the stage in the 1670s and 1680s but lasted much longer in the public imagination, were too brittle for a society realizing that married couples needed to find a way for the marriage to outlast the honeymoon. And the heroic love-versus-honour dilemmas of tragicomedy simply seemed irrelevant to many spectators, a figment of a bygone imagination. Thomas Southerne's *The Wives Excuse* (1692) was the first and best of these new-style marriage plays – a loose, largely unplotted series of open-plan, freeform scenes structured around social gatherings. In Act 1, the Friendalls' marriage is exposed as a sham. Mrs Friendall is faithful, but her husband deserves to be cuckolded. Through a ruse contrived by Lovemore, who has Ruffle insult Friendall with a box on the ears (thus is tragicomic swordplay domesticated), he is exposed as a coward, provoking this speech from his wife:

> How despicable a condition must that matrimony be, when the husband, whom we look upon as a sanctuary for a woman's honour, must be obliged to the discretion and management of a wife for the security of his own! Have a care of thinking that way; for, in a married state, as in the public, we tie ourselves up, indeed, but to be protected in our persons, fortunes and honours by those very laws that restrain us in other things; for few will obey, but for the benefit they receive from the government. (Southerne 1995: 2.2.79–86)

A few talking points there! This is a neat restatement of the contractual basis of monarchical reign, such as had just been achieved under the Revolution settlement.

Such plays were anchored firmly in bourgeois domestic circumstances as opposed to the frequently exotic locations of tragicomedy. They don't threaten their characters with loss of life, moving instead towards a socially engineered rather than a miraculous happy ending, firmly based on the upholding of moral norms. The problem at the core of *Love's Last Shift* is how to shore up a marriage against the threat of predatory male appetite: how to combat the orthodoxy handed down from Restoration sex-comedies that marriage is an inherently tedious, unnatural and unsustainable institution. It dramatizes the final-act repentance of a bankrupt gamester, the whoring drunken rake Loveless, who has abandoned his wife Amanda but on returning home is tricked into bedding her under the pretence that she is a top-class whore. The play's famous repentance/conversion scene deploys a quasi-religious language of virtue and holy martyrdom that we have seen operating in early tragicomedy. The assumption that good will triumph over evil, that vicious men are capable of being permanently converted to goodness – these assumptions are domesticated from the happy endings of tragicomedy.

Plays that end happily, such as Steele's *The Tender Husband* (1705) and *The Conscious Lovers* (1722), were trading on forms of pathos as sentimental as those that fuelled the tragedies. *The Conscious Lovers* illustrates the kind of comedy increasingly desired by a middle class that wanted to see flattering portraits of itself in credible action. Although it uses tragicomic memes, such as the restoring of Indiana's true identity as Sealand's estranged daughter, much of it is concerned with policing proper sexual behaviour. An aspect of the play's redefinition of gentility is that the duel between Myrtle and Young Bevil, that in a tragicomedy would have led at least to the wounding of one party, is called off. Heroic intrigue tragedies and Roman or pseudo-classical tragedies written in the epic strain were still being staged well into the eighteenth century, however – and it was to plays such as those that the high plots of tragicomedies migrated. They were given new impetus by the phenomenal success of Ambrose Philips's *The Distrest Mother* (1712) and Joseph Addison's *Cato* (1713). Between the Scylla of pseudo-classical tragedy and the Charybdis of sentimental comedy, tragicomedy found itself squeezed out.

Tragicomedy Parodied

Very few plays identified as tragicomedies were written in the eighteenth century. From 1750 onwards, virtually all of them are adaptations of Shakespeare, Fletcher or Massinger and Field. Up until mid-century, most of those that were so called were satires or parodies. John Philips's two plays satirizing the 1715 Jacobite uprising, published by the notorious Edmund Curll, are good examples. *The earl of Mar marr'd. with the humours of Jockey, the Highlander: a tragi-comical farce* (1715), treats us to cod-Scots albeit sounding more like north-east English dialect such as this:

> 1 *Mob.* Ken ye *Jonnee* with what muckle deal of Spreet the General talks: He's a reeght Lad Ise warrant ye. He'll stuff the Deel's Weam full of *Englishmen*, or else Ise be as dead a Mon, as *Jenny* that hong in a Coord fro killing her Bearne with an auld rusty Durk. (Philips 1715: 2)

Philips followed this up with *The pretender's flight; or, a mock coronation. With the humours of the facetious Harry St. John, a tragi-comical farce* (1716), the principal target being Henry St. John, Lord Bolingbroke – he who left England to serve the Pretender at his 'court' in St. Germain, a traitor in Philips's eyes. The designation 'tragi-comical farce' was an attempt to cash in on the success of John Gay's *The What D'Ye Call It: a Tragi-Comi-Pastoral Farce* that opened on 23 February 1715. Pope, who may have been involved in the writing, estimated that Gay made around £100 from box-office takings, and he sold the copyright for just over £16. Like Buckingham's *Rehearsal*, as well as being hilarious in its own right, *The What D'Ye Call It* is an extremely sophisticated meditation on the theatrical landscape and on generic miscegenation.

Amateur dramatics are taking place in the Hall of a Country Justice's house '*adorn'd with Scutcheons and Stag's Horns*' (Gay 1983: vol. 1, 179). The performance is prefaced by some fussing about costume reminiscent of Shakespeare's mechanicals and a discussion between Sir Roger and his Steward about the nature of the play he has commissioned. He is adamant that there should be a ghost and that the play must be a tragedy *and* a comedy, though 'I would have it a Pastoral too: and if you could make it a Farce, so much the better – and what if you crown'd all with a Spice of your Opera?' (ll. 54–6). The play that follows manages somehow to fill this bill. Thomas Filbert, played by Sir Roger's son Thomas, is promised to Kitty Carrot (played by the Steward's daughter Kitty) but has made Dorcas pregnant. A recruiting sergeant is eager to press him to the wars, and in his predicament he is not unwilling to go. This situation is resolved when it becomes clear that Dorcas's child is in fact the Squire's, leaving Thomas and Kitty free to marry. The twist here is that their offstage marriage is a genuine ceremony. They have tricked the Squire by marrying for real. The second plot hangs on Dorcas's brother, Timothy Peascod, who as the action opens has been cashiered for desertion and is to be executed imminently. In 2.2, Peascod makes a full confession of all his pathetic misdemeanours which he thinks to be grave crimes. The rhetoric rises to its tragic climax when he is given a copy of *Pilgrim's Progress* to comfort him:

PEASCOD.
Lend me thy Handkercher—*The Pilgrim's Pro—*
[*Reads and weeps.*
—*The Pilgrim's Progress—Eighth—Edi-ti-on*
Lon-don—Prin-ted—for Ni-cho-las Bod-ding-ton:
With new Ad-di-tions never made before
—Oh! 'tis so moving, I can read no more.
[*Drops the Book.*
(2.1.24–8)

Strangely, Peascod's naïve reading of the publisher's blurb from the front matter of *Pilgrim's Progress* is as sad as it is simultaneously hilarious. After a sentimental scene with his daughter Joyce, Peascod is led away and just as he is taking leave of all his friends, a sudden entirely random reprieve is announced – a device that Gay would reuse in *The Beggar's Opera* (1728). The pastoral aspect of Sir Roger's commission is fulfilled when, for example, Kitty has worked herself into a screaming fit and is doused in cold water by a Grandmother and an Aunt, characters parodying the mature women who feature in Shakespeare's histories. Kitty's reaction is to imagine a great flood, expressed in mind-boggling pastoral/georgic imagery:

> Hah! – I am turn'd a Stream – look all below;
> It flows, and flows, and will for ever flow.
> The Meads are all afloat – the Haycocks swim.
> Hah! who comes here? – my *Filbert!* drown not him.
> Bagpipes in Butter, Flocks in fleecy Fountains,
> Churns, Sheep-hooks, Seas of Milk, and honey Mountains.
> (2.8.80–5)

The action is punctuated with songs and ballads, its Epilogue pronouncing this moral:

> *Our Stage Play has a Moral – and no doubt*
> *You all have Sense enough to find it out.*

My readers no doubt have sense enough to know that this action is a comic skit on the theatre of the preceding age. In 3.3, a series of ghosts appears to Sir Roger and two other magistrates. In *Macbeth*-like sequence, the apparitions accuse the bench of their abuses of justice. The fourth ghost is that of an embryo, 'begot before my Mother married, / Who whipt by you, of me poor Child miscarried' (9–10). Perhaps ghosts don't come more ghostly than embryo's ghosts, though this one gains substance when it goes on to sing a song. Throughout the play, spoofs occur of successful plays by Banks, Lee, Otway, Dryden, Ambrose Philips, Addison and many others. That the operation of chance or 'Fortune' in tragicomedy is a principal target is obvious from Gay's inspired preface to the published edition:

> We have often had Tragi-Comedies upon the *English* Theatre with Success: but in that sort of Composition the Tragedy and Comedy are in distinct Scenes, and may easily be separated from each other. But the whole Art of the Tragi-Comi-Pastoral Farce lies in the interweaving the several Kinds of the Drama with each other, so that they cannot be distinguish'd or separated. (Gay 1983: vol. 1, 174)

Gay goes on to tabulate a series of objections against his play as a tragedy, in which the question of an embryo's ghost looms large; followed by a series of objections against it as a comedy, in which the question of an embryo's ghost looms large. The two sets are perfectly self-cancelling.

4

Modern Tragicomedy

Melodrama as 'Second Stage' Tragicomedy

As Buckingham's *Rehearsal* marks a sceptical moment in the history of tragicomedy, so *The What D'Ye Call It* writes its epitaph. Where does tragicomedy go? There is a plausible argument to be made, though it can only be lightly touched upon here, that it surfaces in nineteenth-century melodrama. In August 1802, Henry Harris (son of the Covent Garden Theatre manager Thomas Harris), wrote to the dramatist Frederick Reynolds reporting on an entirely novel species of entertainment called melodrama, that mixed the drama with the *ballet* of action. Romantic and sensational in plot and punctuated by music, early melodrama is a *mixed* entertainment form. Such mixing can be understood in terms of the discussion of mixed modes that has been omnipresent in this book.

If melodrama might be usefully understood as a second stage of tragicomedy, we must immediately concede that the line of transmission is indirect. Early 'importers' of the new art from Paris such as Henry Harris do speak of it as constituted by mingling of forms, but they do not give it the label tragicomedy. And this mixedness takes us as far as we can get from the insistence on *vraisemblance*: precisely because mixedness was inappropriate to the sense of proper representation and 'violent to our imagination' it offered the desirable possibility of an engagement with the sublime. 'Melodrama' is finally produced by the violent generic intermixture and experimentation of the later eighteenth century, and draws elements from German *Sturm und Drang*, monodrama, opera and the *drame*, all of which are themselves employing tragicomic techniques, structures and modes. Visually, its legacy is the long history of pantomime and Italian *commedia*, whereas tragicomedy is plausibly a source of its management of plot and dialogue. By systematically alternating between tragic and comic modes within scenes and even within character, melodrama can be seen to extend and consolidate tragicomedy's basic admixture of forms. Its two main root stocks in the late eighteenth century were sentimental comedy and gothic or popular tragedy, which could be late-eighteenth-century heirs to the two strains that meet in tragicomedy: the essentially comic 'drama of the second chance' leading from Shakespeare to sentimental comedy, and that fundamentally tragic drama of fate, dissonant shifts in register, and emphatic class separation leading from Fletcher into Dryden. In the present book's terms, we can observe replicated in melodramas such as Dion Boucicault's *The Colleen Bawn or The Brides of Garryowen* (1860) and *The Shaughraun* (1874) several of the memes that characterize Fletcherian tragicomedy.

Boucicault has some claim to be nicknamed 'the dramatist of resurrection'. An entire scene in *The Shaughraun*, 3.4, takes place during the vagabond [shaughraun] Conn O'Kelly's wake. Conn, who has already resurrected several times in the play, is not dead yet – merely attending his own funeral; and the action is beautifully positioned between tragedy and farce, apparent in this set of stage directions:

> *A shot is fired from the hogshead.* KINCHELA *throws up his hands, staggers, falls.* MOYA *utters a cry and falls on her knees, covering her face with her hands. The hogshead*

> *rises a little – advances to* MOYA, *and covers her like an extinguisher. The legs of* CONN *have been seen under the barrel as it moves.* (Boucicault 1987: 323)

This is one of the tragicomic 'blended scenes' that we have been identifying: a perfect manipulation of the hilarious and the affecting. In *The Colleen Bawn*, the tragicomic turn is obvious in Boucicault's manipulation of a novelized version of a true crime story that was his source. The real event was the cruel murder in 1819 of a farmer's daughter, Ellen Hanley, by her husband John Scanlan and his confederate servant, Stephan Sullivan. The playwright's most significant alteration of the source story was to bring Eily O'Connor, his 'colleen bawn' (fair girl) back from the dead. Having been thrown from a rock by Danny Mann, the deformed, ultra-devoted and misguided servant of Hardress Cregan, she is rescued by the poacher Myles-na-Coppaleen and 'resurrected' in time to have her secret husband Cregan acquitted of her murder. Boucicault has therefore turned the tragic events of his source into a tragicomedy (Figure 10).

The play's mechanics are those of crossed love, as is typical in tragicomedy. Anne Chute is promised to Hardress Cregan, but he is married secretly to Eily O'Connor, whose Irish brogue and simple country manners make Cregan unwilling to face the social stigma of owning her for his wife. In performance, of course, the Colleen's naïve simplicity is turned into irresistible charm acting as a critique of Cregan's *snobisme*. We can see it as a version of the 'supernatural virtue' meme familiar from tragicomedy. Myles-na-Coppaleen, the loveable rogue played by Boucicault himself, might be compared to Falstaffian characters such as Fletcher's humorous lieutenant; but he is also one of the play's 'Protector' figures. This play deploys the 'supernatural' rather less than does, say, Boucicault's earlier *The Corsican Brothers* (1852), the sensationalism of which derives from the paranormal effects of second sight, but folk-myth and the atmospheric accretions of particular landscapes are powerfully present. True to its origins, the play makes

Figure 10 *Dunloe Cottage, Co. Kerry in 1907, called the 'cottage of the Colleen Bawn' to capitalise on Boucicault's play. Photo by Topical Press Agency/Getty Images.*

great use of songs, of background music and of sensation scenes issuing in stage pictures: the theatrecraft involved in the 'murder' of Eily, followed by Myles's shooting of Danny and his fishing of Eily from the water, whether alive or dead the audience does not at that point know, is of considerable complexity. Such involved deployment of theatre arts can also be traced in tragicomedy, whence it is imported from masque. It is not, however, aimed at the same relatively elevated section of society, and that is a very considerable difference.

The previous chapters have traced the continuous history in English drama of the term 'tragicomedy'. We have seen that the form was at its most active in the period between the early 1600s and the early 1700s; and that for reasons discussed in the preceding chapter, the artistic and commercial needs that brought tragicomedy into existence came to be felt no longer. If we could read every play published in eighteenth-century England, some would be found that have not been identified as tragicomedies but are best catalogued under that descriptor. As a broad generalization, however, the cultural appetites that made tragicomedy theatrically popular had been assuaged. The suggestion has been put that tragicomedy finds an afterlife in melodrama, a form specializing in the kinds of *coup de théâtre* that occur in tragicomedy, and in averting danger at the last moment. By and large, though, danger is not averted by means of resurrection; and the happy ending is achieved not by a protector figure but by a narrative detail finally finding its expression. My examples drawn from Boucicault, a canny writer who knew his theatre history, might be as close as the two forms ever come.

This chapter therefore abandons the historical methodology of earlier chapters, as well as the emphasis on English drama, to concentrate on moments and dramatists whose apprehension of experience challenges the adequacy of the traditional major forms to represent it. In historical terms, tragicomedy was a form devised to provide a more adequate representation of the complexity of experience: lived experience often provided human beings with mixed outcomes, or some human beings with happy outcomes and others with miserable fates, as we saw in *The Visit*, with a vengeance. Ultimately, it was a theatrical means of helping audiences and readers to explore and comprehend such seeming injustice. More recent tragicomedy maintains the objective of doing justice to the complexity of experience, though the resolution is no longer seen primarily in religious or providential terms. In modern times, tragicomedy is revived to serve the needs of audiences who have lost their religious, moral and emotional bearings.

Ibsen: *The Wild Duck* (1884)

Though tragicomedy was 'squeezed out' in the eighteenth century and the term fell into disuse, what we have called the 'memes' that characterize the form, the parabolas of dramatic action that comprise it and the theatrical devices that it deploys did not die overnight. Danny Mann, principal evil-doer in *The Colleen Bawn*, is a heavily sentimentalized version of the shadow-casting dastardly villain featured in some melodramas. And that shadow is still being cast in the drama of Henrik Ibsen (1828–1906), even in those dramas celebrated for their formal realism. In Act 3 of *The Wild Duck*, the domestic happiness of the Ekdal family is interrupted by a fateful knocking at the door. Enter Haakon Werle, the play's principal villain:

There is a knock on the front door.

Hedvig Mother, someone's knocking.

Hjalmar Oh, now that's going to start.

Gina Let me take care of it.

She goes over, opens the door and steps back in surprise.

Oh! Oh, no!

Haakon Werle, *in a fur-lined coat with a fur collar, takes a step into the room.*

I beg your pardon, but I believe my son is living in this house. (Ibsen 1980: 174)

Continuities with melodrama are equally obvious in *A Doll's House* (1879) and *Ghosts* (1882), complicating the sense that there is any clean break between unnatural and exaggerated melodrama on the one hand, and realism/naturalism on the other.

George Bernard Shaw (1856–1950) was one of the most important mediators of Ibsen's plays in establishing an English understanding of them. In his seminal essay *The Quintessence of Ibsenism* (1891, third edition 1913), he reads Ibsen's *The Wild Duck* (1884) as 'a tragi-comic slaughtering of sham Ibsenism' (Shaw 1948: 75). This initiated an influential reading of the play as a satiric repudiation of his own followers, the 'Ibsenites'. Gregers Werle, the misguided zealot whose mission is to puncture 'idealism' by exposing the shabby truth concealed by the Ekdals' supposedly happy marriage, becomes a version of Ibsen himself – the idealist as interfering busybody, a version of himself that the real Ibsen has outgrown and now wishes only to ridicule. Shaw reviewed a production at the Globe in May 1897: 'to look on with horror and pity at a profound tragedy, shaking with laughter all the time at an irresistible comedy' (McFarlane 1970: 168–9). Later, in 'Tolstoy: Tragedian or Comedian?' (1921), Shaw extended the argument to all of Ibsen's plays, calling him 'the dramatic poet who firmly established tragicomedy as a much deeper and grimmer entertainment than tragedy' (qtd. in Carlson 1984: 309). There is authorial warrant for the idea that *The Wild Duck*, at any rate, was intended as a tragicomedy. Ibsen himself called it that in an interview given on 3 April 1898: 'it is to be a tragi-comedy ... or else Hedvig's death is incomprehensible' (McFarlane 1970: 169). So what do we understand by this designation in the late nineteenth century? How is a play in which a fourteen-year-old girl shoots herself anything other than a tragedy?

One backdrop to Ibsen's theatrical consideration of idealism is provided by discussions of realism *versus* idealism in European theatre theory and practice. François Ponsard's play *Lucrèce* (1843), introducing a school of drama to be known as the *école de bon sens*, launched a new concern with realistic depiction of actual society, moving away from inflexible Germanic metaphysical idealism. Dumas *fils* took up the école's objectives in plays such as *La Dame aux camélias* (1851) wherein he insisted that drama must retain its moral purpose, however far its technique should move in the direction of 'slice of life' realism. Such didacticism was challenged by Émile Zola, who, in his essay on Dumas entitled *Nos auteurs dramatiques* (1881), concludes: 'Dumas ... is in the idealist school. The world as he sees it seems badly constructed, and he feels a constant need to rebuild it' (qtd. in Carlson 1984: 274). Dumas wishes to be a moralist and a legislator; Zola moves towards the role of 'scientific' and objective observer. Ibsen himself often asserted the realist credentials of his plays and denied that they had any moralistic tendency; for example, in a letter to Sophus Scharndorph of 6 January 1882 in respect of *Ghosts*: 'My intention was to try and give the reader the impression of experiencing a piece of reality. But nothing would more effectively run counter to this intention than asserting the author's opinions into the dialogue' (McFarlane 1970: 94). The preface that Strindberg wrote for *Miss Julie* (1888) and the play itself provide clear vantage points on such debates. The preface is shot through with social Darwinist theories about survival, repeating Ibsen's obsession with heredity, offering environmental, physiological and psychological possibilities for contextualizing the play's action. Remarks on genre ridicule the phrase 'the joy of living' that echoes through Ibsen's play *Ghosts* (1881). There can be 'joy' in tragedy, Strindberg allows, but not the trivial pleasure desired by Ibsen's characters. Strindberg writes: 'I find the "joy of life" in life's cruel and mighty conflicts' (Strindberg 1976: 93). One such conflict is the class warfare between Miss Julie and Jean represented in the play. Against this background, the contest between realism and idealism in *The Wild Duck* might almost be read as an allegory of the debate over the direction that theatre itself should take.

This is the superheated atmosphere into which *The Wild Duck* lands. In the kind of life led by the Ekdals, there may be found a tragic dignity but, in the broad details of their existence, they behave as the foolish characters in a comedy. The play stages a battle for possession of Hjalmar Ekdal's soul. On one side is Gregers Werle, proponent of the 'claim of the ideal', who requires Ekdal to confront the truth about his marriage: that his wife, Gina, is the cast-off mistress of Werle's rich father Haakon, and that his daughter Hedvig is Werle Senior's illegitimate child. On the other is Dr Relling, cynical 'realist' and proponent of the 'saving lie', who has gifted Ekdal the idea that he is a talented photographer capable someday of an invention that will revolutionize the craft. The attic above the house has been developed as an adventure playground for Old Ekdal, Hjalmar's disgraced father who has taken the rap for breaches of forest laws when in partnership in a timber business with Werle Senior. Lieutenant Ekdal is a figure of fun, ludicrously dressed in his military uniform and a 'dirty, reddish-brown wig', shooting rabbits in his Lilliputian hunting-ground. In that fantasy space also, a wounded wild duck is being nursed back to health as a family project. All of the major characters are situated in relation to the maimed bird, that therefore functions symbolically, compensating for the under-ambitiousness of realist conventions by enabling a subtextual realm in which the play can mean more than it ever says. Lest the audience fail to perceive this, Ibsen somewhat heavy-handedly writes the method into the text:

> **Gina** (*thoughtfully, her sewing in her lap*) Wasn't that a funny thing, saying he'd like to be a dog?
>
> **Hedvig** You know, mother – I think when he said that he meant something else.
>
> **Gina** What could he mean?
>
> **Hedvig** I don't know. But I felt as though he meant something different from what he was saying all the time.
>
> **Gina** You think so? Yes, it certainly was strange. (Ibsen 1980: 153–4; Ibsen [1950] 1965: 185)

Hedvig is the victim of that subtextual realm. She understands from Gregers that sacrificing the wild duck will bring back her father's love for her by showing the strength of her own. She goes the extra step and sacrifices herself (Figure 11).

Ibsen's handling of what Mary McCarthy calls 'the small shocking event, the psychopathology of everyday life' (qtd. in McFarlane 1970: 277) is illustrated in Hjalmar's frequently risible behaviour, his vanity and egotism that would be comical

Figure 11 *Richard Piper (Old Ekdal) and Sara West (Hedwig) in* The Wild Duck *directed by Simon Stone, Barbican, London, 2014. Photo by robbie jack/Corbis via Getty Images.*

if they were not wreaking such havoc on his family. In Act 2, he has asked his wife to bring him his coat:

> **Hjalmar** (*stretches*) Ah, now I feel more at home. Loose-fitting clothes suit my figure better. Don't you think, Hedvig?
>
> **Hedvig** Yes, father.
>
> **Hjalmar** When I loosen my tie so that the ends flow like this – Look! What do you think of that?
>
> **Hedvig** Oh, yes, that looks very good with your moustache and those big curls of yours.
>
> **Hjalmar** I wouldn't call them curls. Waves.
>
> **Hedvig** Yes, they're such big curls.
>
> **Hjalmar** They are waves. (Ibsen 1980: 141; Ibsen [1950] 1965: 170–1)

Just after this, it transpires that Hjalmar has forgotten his promise to bring something back for Hedvig from his fancy dinner, disappointing her by producing only a printed card bearing the menu. This, in a family where the women only have a hot meal when Hjalmar is present. In Act 3, Hedvig, who is going blind, offers to retouch some photographs for her father, an offer he accepts despite his awareness that it could further damage her sight. Small-scale betrayals are juxtaposed with grandiose rhetoric to render Hjalmar Ekdal risible, contemptible and pitiable by turns.

As the play moves towards its sad finale, there are lengthy stretches of action capable of making audiences giggle uncomfortably, if not exactly laugh out loud. Almost in the manner of a Wagnerian *leitmotif*, Ibsen deploys tiny details to thread a comic tone throughout the solemnity of the action. Thus in Act 3, Old Ekdal suddenly enters from the attic with a rabbit skin, and Relling proposes a toast to the 'old hunter' (I use Ellis-Fermor's older translation here, because it is a little more pointed):

> **Hjalmar** [*touching glasses with him*]. Yes. To the sportsman on the brink of the grave.
>
> **Relling** To the grey-haired – [*drinking*] ... But tell me, is it grey his hair is, or white?
>
> **Hjalmar** It's actually betwixt and between. As a matter of fact, he hasn't much hair left, in any case. (Ibsen [1950] 1965: 207)

This of course recapitulates the ludicrous glimpse of Hjalmar's popinjay vanity quoted above. Hair is a leitmotif that can be lightly sounded for comic effect, as when, in Act 4, Hjalmar threatens to wring the wild duck's neck in his distraught daughter's hearing:

> **Hjalmar** [*pausing*]. I tell you I will spare it – for your sake. It shall not be hurt; not a hair of its – well, as I said, I will spare it. (Ibsen [1950] 1965: 216)

A script teetering on the brink of the hilarious and the melancholy continues as Relling conjures up a picture of Hjalmar's idyllic family life, punctured by Gina's uneducated malapropism – 'don't sit there making an aspersion of me' – leading Hjalmar into a sentimentalized fantasy about the good life his invention will surely provide for his beloved Hedvig, whose birthday will be celebrated in the attic on the following day. Relling's word-painting of a 'happy family circle' is rudely erased by Werle's sudden talk of 'swamp vapour', the symbolic stench of which cannot be removed by Gina's literal-minded talk of 'airing' the house. Suspecting that 'the claim of the ideal' may again raise its ugly head, Relling threatens to throw Werle downstairs, just as a fateful knock at the door introduces the melodramatic figure of Werle Senior '*dressed in a fur coat*', referred to at the start of this section. It is a rich passage, uncertain in tone, carefully poised between the comic surface and the resonant bass notes of a tragedy waiting to happen.

How far does the play's ending justify calling it a tragicomedy? The discovery of Hedvig's body, Hjalmar's momentary belief that she is alive, his exaggerated reaction when he knows that she is dead – self-accusatory breast-beating, imploring the heavens – the mother and father carrying off her body: all of these details create a histrionic and in Hjalmar's case near-parodic version of *King Lear*, just as earlier passages on blindness have brought *Oedipus* to mind. The play does not end with Hedvig's death. The antagonists Relling and Werle are left onstage. If the audience sees any refuge in the possibility that Hedvig's death was accidental, not suicide, as Werle has a vested interest in doing, that possibility is immediately squashed by the man of science. At once, Werle turns the death into an efficacious sacrifice: 'Hedvig has not died in vain. Did you see how grief set free all that is most noble in him?' (Ibsen 1980: 216). Remorselessly, Relling rejects that escape also: 'In nine months, little Hedvig will be nothing more to him than a theme for a recitation.' The play closes with an enigmatic statement from Werle to the effect that his destiny is to be 'thirteenth at table' – as Hjalmar actually was in the dinner party that opens the play. In Norwegian, the play's final line is given to Dr Relling: 'Å fan' tro det', for which a contemporary translation would be 'Oh fuck it'. Something depends on translation for the final effect left on the audience. Meyer's version ends with a stage direction: 'Relling *laughs and spits*.' He tries to render the phatic force of Relling's curse. In David Eldridge's 2005 version, Relling's line observes period decorum: 'Damn you' (Ibsen 2005: 113). The Ellis-Fermor translation closes on an open-ended and unfinished phrase from Relling: 'I wonder …' (Ibsen [1950] 1965: 260). This leaves an audience wondering what Relling wonders. Whether or not Werle has the courage to commit suicide? We are already sceptical about suicide. We have heard Hjalmar posturingly refer to himself in the third person about the hour in which 'Hjalmar Ekdal held the pistol to his own heart' but 'in that moment of supreme trial I won the victory over myself' (202). Any association with Hjalmar would leave an audience doubting Werle's seriousness of purpose. Even suicide can be a risible subject in this play. Open-endedly poised between suicidal nihilism and the reductive cynicism of Relling's 'saving lie' the play ends.

The philosophical territory occupied by Ibsen, the terrain that he uses tragicomic form to explore, is announced early in the nineteenth century by 'pessimistic' philosophers such as Arthur Schopenhauer. In *The World as Will and Representation* [*Idea*] (1819, revised 1844), Schopenhauer says this:

> The life of every individual ... is really always a tragedy, but gone through in detail it has the character of a comedy. For the deeds and vexations of the day, the restless irritation of the moment, the desires and fears of the week, the mishaps of every hour, are all through chance, which is ever bent upon some jest, scenes of a comedy. But the never-satisfied wishes, the frustrated efforts, the hopes unmercifully crushed by fate ... are always a tragedy. (Schopenhauer 1966: 1: 322)

If this were a description of *The Wild Duck*, it could scarcely be more accurate. Ibsen's ambiguity of tone results from the characters' failure to bring their actions into line with the aspirations expressed in their speech. Tragicomedy in Ibsen's hands has a satirical tendency, valued for its ability to hold absurdity and social displacement in tension with lofty idealism.

Chekhov: *The Cherry Orchard* (1904)

Anton Pavlovich Chekhov (1860–1904) was less indebted than was Ibsen to theoretical debate about the theatre's position in society – and of course he had the benefit of reading Ibsen's work. (*The Wild Duck* was translated into Russian in 1892.) The 1860s had been an active period in Russian theatre theory. Chernyshevsky championed a theatre informed by scientific materialism and social progress, opposed by Grigoriev who advocated a return to German transcendental ways of thinking and commitment to a drama deriving from the collective consciousness of the people. Subsequently, there had been little structural disagreement. Regarding Chekhov's theatre practice, the most significant development was the foundation in 1897 of the Moscow Art Theatre, dedicated to realistic acting, ensemble playing, detailed research behind the productions' scenic systems and reformed lighting practices. The turn of the century saw the birth of what has been termed a 'silver age' in Russian aesthetics, when art as an explicit vehicle for social and political criticism was rejected. Chekhov preferred to think of himself as an objective and detached observer of life. His *Cherry Orchard* finds a place in this discussion not because he or anyone else at the time called the play a 'tragicomedy', but because, in retrospect, that is the best way of describing its distinctive atmospheric blend. Unlike all of the plays so far examined in this book, the characters here are not placed in mortal danger. No one dies, is in danger of dying or is miraculously saved from death, but it could be argued that an entire imagined community faces extinction.

There can seldom have been a play that provoked more fundamental disagreement between its author and its first director than Chekhov's *The Cherry Orchard*. Famously, that disagreement with Konstantin Stanislavski was about genre. Chekhov several times referred to his play in the making as a light comedy. When the play was no more than an idea, Chekhov repeatedly referred to it as 'very funny', a 'comedy', a 'vaudeville' and a 'farce'; 'merry and frivolous' (Chekhov 1974–83: vol. 11, 14, 15, 246; Styan 1978: 239). 'Vaudeville' in the Russian theatrical tradition is a precise term for a nineteenth-century form adapted from French prototypes and Russian comic opera, popular in the mid-nineteenth century for its acerbic social commentary. He tried to steer

Nemirovich-Danchenko, co-director of the Moscow Art Theatre, away from the tragic end of the spectrum, sometimes in detail: 'I am afraid Ania may speak in a tearful tone [that is, afraid that she will be made to speak in such a tone] ... Ania doesn't weep, not even once, nowhere speaks in a tearful voice, in the second act she has tears in the eyes but the tone is cheerful, lively' (23 October 1903; Chekhov 1974–83: vol. 11, 283–4). Stanislavski continued to deny categorically that the play was a comedy. It made him cry like a woman, he said, and was a tragedy for the ordinary man. Stanislavski never appreciated that it was not necessarily a tragedy just because the play made him weep, or because characters in the play weep.

The play had its first performance on 17 January 1904. It was immediately obvious to its author that the production was paced as a *drame*: a serious play or even a tragedy. The great director Meyerhold perhaps came closest to understanding the uncertainties of Chekhovian tone when he noted its melodramatic undernotes and compared it to Chekhov's symbolist contemporary Maeterlinck:

> Your play is abstract, like a symphony by Tchaikovsky. And the stage director must first of all catch this with his ear. In the 3d act, against the background of silly clattering – it is this 'clattering' which is to be heard by people – unnoticed/ imperceptibly in comes the Horror. ... merriment, in which the sounds of death can be heard. In this act there is something of Maeterlinck, something horrible. (8 May 1904; Meyerhold 1968: 78)

J. L. Styan asks the question how the play can 'allow either the heroics of prophecy or the melodrama of dispossession' and rightly answers in terms of its 'contribution to an embracing structure of comi-tragic ambivalence' (Styan 1978: 246–7). Tragicomedy in Chekhov's hands is a dramaturgy capable of bringing out the ambivalence and undecidability of characters in specific social circumstances. Like Ludwig Wittgenstein's iconic duck–rabbit analogy, Chekhov's situations can be perceived simultaneously as funny and melancholy, or one or the other depending on their theatrical presentation and on the audience's perspective.

Stanislavski had no tradition of tragicomedy within which to understand Chekhov's theatrical experiment. In this respect, British theatregoers were from the earliest days at an advantage. The first available translation into English of *Cherry Orchard* was published by George Calderon (1912), already used for a production by the Incorporated Stage Society in 1911. Although Calderon was disparaging about this production in intrusive footnotes to his translation, both it and Calderon's influential introduction to *Two Plays by Tchekof* set the agenda for understanding Chekhov in the following decades. Calderon argued that Chekhov's plays were 'centrifugal', not 'self-centred': they articulate group, not individual, emotions. Words are spoken for the 'atmosphere' rather than to express individual character. Suffering results from conditions over which individuals have little control, rather than from evil intentions or actions. As for their genre, they are mingled – tragicomedies, though he does not use the word. 'Life is never pure comedy or pure tragedy', argued Calderon.

> The Universe does not stand still in awe of our private successes or misfortunes ... Seeking as he did to throw our eyes outwards from the individual destiny, to discover its relation to surrounding Life, he habitually mingled tragedy (which is Life seen close at hand) with comedy (which is Life seen from a distance.) His plays are tragedies with the texture of comedy'. (Chekhov 1912: 14)

English audiences were early attuned to understanding Chekhov's portrayal of life's fluidity and elusiveness. Shaw was an early convert, as witness his introduction to the 1919 edition of *Heartbreak House*. From the 1920s onwards, when Chekhov was taken up by Katherine Mansfield, Virginia Woolf and other luminaries, leading to publication of his notebook, diary and letters – scholarly interest cemented by visits from the Moscow Art Theatre in 1928 and 1931 – English theatregoers were receptive to his tragicomic treatment of the complexity of existence.

Compared to *The Wild Duck*, *Cherry Orchard* embraces a wider section of society, though its rural setting necessarily excludes much that was historically significant in the Russia of Chekhov's period; and if the student Trofimov goes in for, in Styan's words, 'the heroics of prophecy' (Styan 1978: 245), the play is nevertheless far from being prophetic. The final decades of the nineteenth century saw a massive industrialization programme in Russia that brought with it the formation of an urban proletariat. The only signs of that in the play are the '*line of telegraph poles, and ... the vague outlines of a large town*' described in the set for Act 2. Within a year of production, the failed revolution of 1905 would have taken place, though the play itself predicts only a gentle, inexorable transfer of an insolvent estate into the hands of the former serf Lopakhin. The latter is a 'businessman', a property developer who speaks of having profited from planting poppies, but to what class fraction he now belongs is difficult to pinpoint. Since the 87-year-old manservant Firs is as near as we come to a serf, one who regards the 1861 Emancipation Act as a great disaster, the play tells us little about how peasants actually live at the turn of the century, or the unrest that troubled agrarian areas of the country, until a drunk and shabby 'Passer-By' (Hingley translation: Chekhov [1964] 2008: 268; called a 'Tramp' by Fen: Chekhov [1951] 1970) behaves with comic insolence in Act 2. Trofimov is a particularly interesting case of undecidability. Since the 1880s, the universities had been breeding a revolutionary intelligentsia whose importance in disseminating early Marxism and fomenting the politics of the 1900s would be critical. Is Trofimov of that ilk? He is given his 'prophetic' speech at the close of Act 2, but his sentiments can as easily be compared to Hjalmar Ekdal's brand of idealism as to pre-revolutionary fervour:

> To rid ourselves of the pettiness and the illusions which stop us being free and happy, that's the whole meaning and purpose of our lives. Forward then! We are marching triumphantly on towards that bright star shining there far away. On, on! No falling back, my friends. (Chekhov [1964] 2008: 269)

Trofimov's callow prudishness and lack of worldly experience emerges in his confrontation with Madame Ranyevskaia the landowner (as she is called in Elizaveta Fen's 1951 translation: Chekhov ([1951] 1970); more prosaically called Mrs Ranevsky by Ronald Hingley: Chekhov [1964] 2008), to whom he is attracted despite having captivated her young daughter Anya with his rhetoric. One brief exchange between them speaks volumes: of his relationship with Anya, Trofimov orates: 'We are above love.' To which Liubov Andreyeevna satirically replies: 'While I'm supposed to be beneath it, I imagine' (Hingley translation: Chekhov [1964] 2008: 275). Their relationship breaks into open hostility when Liuba undermines his manhood with references to his lack of beard and sexual immaturity: 'You're not above love, you're just what our friend Firs calls a nincompoop' (277). This is a good example of Chekhov's technique of undercutting, taking the ground away from beneath any character tempted to posture or attitudinize.

As the play progresses, characters sometimes speak in a modified soliloquy, revealing aspects of their past biography or their future hopes, seeming to speak *past* rather than *to* other characters even when there are other characters onstage. Occasionally the stage is entirely empty, an effect with enormous theatrical power. Bad fit in the dialogue constantly borders on the comic. When in Act 1 Lopakhin is earnestly explaining his scheme for building on the land freed up by cutting down the cherry orchard, Liubov Andryeevna's response is deliciously beside the point, her main concern being that it's in all the guidebooks. Fen's translation is as follows.

> **Liubov Andryeevna** Cut down? My dear man, forgive me, you don't seem to understand. If there's one thing interesting, one thing really outstanding in the whole country, it's our cherry orchard. (Chekhov [1951] 1970: 343)

Shortly afterwards, her brother Gayev makes his famous apostrophe to his bookcase (Calderon calls it a 'cupboard'): 'For more than a hundred years you have devoted yourself to the highest ideals of goodness and justice' (345). Quarrels and misunderstandings continue until the culminating moment in Act 3 when it transpires that Lopakhin has bought the estate. At the close of Act 2, Trofimov has hectored Ania (Hingley: Anya) over its slave-owing history: 'Don't you see human beings gazing at you from every cherry tree in your orchard, from every leaf and tree-trunk, don't you hear voices?' (368). Now, as Lopakhin triumphantly announces: 'I've bought the very estate where my father and grandfather were serfs, where they weren't even admitted to the kitchen!' (384). Social progress is a comedy for some and a tragedy for others.

Nothing more strongly epitomizes the tragicomic atmosphere of *The Cherry Orchard* than its failed romances. Dooniasha the parlourmaid makes overtures to Liuba's thoroughly objectionable manservant Yasha, a character who shares traits with Strindberg's Jean from *Miss Julie* (1888) – transparently on the make and with no feelings at all. She is loved in turn and in vain by the melancholy, guitar-playing, accident-prone and ridiculous clerk Yepihodov, 'two and twenty misfortunes', whose ludicrously pretentious and verbose idiom is particularly well rendered by Calderon: 'I am a man of cultivation; I have studied various remarkable books, but I cannot fathom the direction of my preferences; do I want to live or do I want to shoot myself, so to speak?' (Chekhov 1912: Act 2). He nevertheless finds himself the only employee retained by Lopakhin when the former owners and their retinue must leave the estate. Outcomes don't necessarily reflect competence in this play. Charlotta is hoping to attract Simeonov-Pishchik, another landowner who is saved from

Figure 12 *Anton Chekhov and his wife, the actress Olga Knipper, in 1900. Photo by Michael Nicholson/Corbis via Getty Images.*

Gayev's fate by the accidental discovery of 'white clay' on his land. The play's purest tragicomic moment occurs in Act 4 when Varia and Lopakhin are deliberately left onstage together so that he can deliver the proposal of marriage expected throughout the action. Since Varia so obviously looks down on this social climber, it is assumed that *she* has been refusing *him*, but given his chance, Lopakhin pointedly fails to take it, leaving Varia sobbing softly. 'When we leave here', says Liuba, 'there won't be a soul in the place' and shortly after that remark, we hear '*the dull thuds of an axe on a tree*' and, for the second time in the play, a sound '*like the sound of a string snapping*' (397–8). However that sound is interpreted, the play's refusal of romance and sentimentality, its equipoise of farce and tragedy, is a prominent aspect of its achievement in a lyrical and poetic form of tragicomedy (Figure 12).

Beckett: *En Attendant Godot/Waiting for Godot* (1953–4)

Waiting for Godot was first published in French in 1953 as *En Attendant Godot.* Beckett's own English translation was published by Grove Press of New York in 1954. In this edition it acquired a subtitle: 'tragicomedy in 2 acts', printed on the dustjacket front. Who gave the play this subtitle and why is something of a mystery in Beckett scholarship. In fact, the earliest occurrence is on the cover of a typescript submitted to the Lord Chamberlain's office on 23 March 1954. The earliest *manuscript* of Beckett's translation does not survive, but it seems unthinkable, given Beckett's meticulous and some would say authoritarian approach to his artistic property, that he was not responsible for this generic ascription and that, if he did not approve, it would have survived onto the flap of the 1956 London edition published by Faber. One reliable account maintains that 'it is safe to assume that Beckett already used [the subtitle] in the first draft of his translation of the play' (Van Hulle and Verhulst 2017: 27). If so, why did he call the play a tragicomedy?

Beckett was an uncommonly erudite dramatist, who had had some significant brushes with tragicomedy early in his life. His biographer James Knowlson tells the story of the burlesque version of Corneille's *Le Cid*, called *Le Kid*, to which Beckett contributed in 1931 as part of the annual production of the Modern Languages Society at Trinity College – not well received by Beckett's colleagues (Knowlson 1996: 122–5). Lovers of French literature are often polarized by admiration for Corneille or admiration for Racine: Beckett was a Racine man and read through his works many times in the course of his life. He was also uncommonly well-versed in English Renaissance drama. Notes he made in 1935 prove that he had recently 'given himself a crash course in Elizabethan and Jacobean drama (Nashe, Peele, Dekker, Marlowe, Marston and Ford)' (Knowlson 1996: 217). One play that made a particular impression on him was John Ford's tragicomedy *The Lovers Melancholy* (1628). In his first play for radio, *All That Fall* (1957), Maddy Rooney, a seventy-year-old Irishwoman, quotes imperfectly a couple of lines from Act 4: 'Sigh out a something something tale of things, Done long ago and ill done' (Beckett 1984: 14). ('Sigh out a lamentable tale of things' is the correct line spoken by Ford's character Meleander.) Beckett's interest in Ford's play might derive from its unusual preoccupation with mental illness taken from Burton's *Anatomy of Melancholy* (1621). It is another tragicomedy that turns on the quasi-incestuous interest of a father and son loving the same woman, as does Fletcher's *The Humorous Lieutenant*, a play also indebted to Burton. But where on earth would Maddy have come across it? As her husband says, 'sometimes one would think you were struggling with a dead language' (34). More on Beckett's language later in the chapter. For the moment, we conclude that Beckett knew what a tragicomedy was and understood much about its history in English and French theatre. So why does he describe *Godot* thus?

The question whether theatre should be an engaged social phenomenon or a politically indifferent aesthetic artefact (committed theatre *versus* 'art for art's sake') is omnipresent in theatre theory stretching back to the late eighteenth century. Bertolt Brecht's theory and practice of 'epic theatre' from the late 1920s onwards, and the controversies to which it gave rise, had given a new lease of life to the argument that theatre must influence the world outside – ideally must seek to *alter* extra-theatrical reality. Even as Brecht was writing, there were those such as Antonin Artaud asking the question where exactly 'reality' resided – whether in the world and its political arrangements or in the Dionysiac darkness that constituted the human psyche. When Beckett was writing *Godot*, thinking about theatre was dominated, inevitably, by the horrors of the Second World War. Written after Hiroshima, it coincides with a ruined Europe trying to recover in a world increasingly dominated by new binary divisions and slogans of 'democracy' and 'socialism'. Dominating the 'social imaginary' was the grotesque deformation of human values in the concentration camps revealed at their liberation and the development of weapons of mass destruction. The play's indebtedness to the conditions Beckett endured as a member of the French resistance has been noted by commentators:

> the most obvious thing about the world of this play [is] that it resembles France occupied by the Germans, in which its author spent the war years. How much waiting must have gone on in that bleak world; how many times must Resistance operatives ... have kept appointments not knowing whom they were to meet ... We can easily see why a Pozzo would be unnerving. (Kenner 1973: 30)

James Knowlson relates *Godot* even more precisely to the awful fate of the Jewish people:

> One of the tramps was first given the Jewish name of Lévy. And Pozzo's treatment of Lucky reminded some of the

> earliest critics of a *capo* in a concentration camp brutalising his victim with his whip. The years just before Beckett wrote *Godot* had seen unimaginable revelations and horrific film footage about the concentration camps of Belsen, Dachau and Auschwitz. (Knowlson 1996: 380–1)

In the theatre, the catastrophe of war produced a crisis specific to the writing of tragedy. In the Greek and Judaeo-Christian tragic tradition, belief in a metaphysical moral order transcending human power had been assumed. Genuine tragic suffering resulted from the exercise of choice, even if, in Greek drama, that was not at all times apparent to the protagonist. Tragedy depends upon the acceptance of responsibility. But this cluster of concepts essential to the definition of tragedy was reduced to absurdity by the experience of global war. If tragedy had been long understood in terms of the struggle for freedom of an individual against overwhelming odds generated by an opposing necessity (fate, destiny), the death-tally of war had made it difficult to consider the suffering or demise of any individual as statistically or otherwise significant. George Steiner in *The Death of Tragedy* (1961) and Raymond Williams in *Modern Tragedy* (1966) were amongst those who argued that 'tragedy' could not have a universal meaning and must be understood against changing contemporary cultural conditions for its structures and specific instantiations. Some creative artists became convinced that such questions were not worth asking because answers to them would not be found. Claude Lanzmann, whose 1985 film *Shoah* dealt with the mass murder of the Jews, has said that he never asked the question *why* the Nazis did what they did, but rather *how*, because asking big questions produces small answers. Beckett's early plays are a theatre of small answers. *Endgame* (1958) begins in dialogue with classical tragedy. Like *Godot*, it begins at its end, with Clov's 'Finished, it's finished, nearly finished, it must be nearly finished' adopting a tactic similar to Estragon's 'Nothing to be done' (Beckett [1958] 1973: 12; Beckett [1956] 1965: 9). Hamm's meditation on the quality of his misery might refer back to misery as represented in the tradition of classical tragedy: 'Can there be misery – (*he yawns*) – loftier than mine? No doubt. Formerly. But now? (*Pause.*) My father? (*Pause.*) My mother?' (12). The passage from Schopenhauer cited in the section on *The Wild Duck* in connection with Ibsen (on 'the restless irritation of the moment') has been seen as relevant to Beckett also. He was deeply versed in Schopenhauer, one of the few philosophers whom he considered entirely readable. In *Falsifying Beckett*, Matthew Feldman considers this passage to be an inspiration for Beckettian tragicomedy as compelling as the Caspar David Friedrich painting *Mann und Frau den Mond betrachend* (Man and Woman observing the Moon) acknowledged by Beckett as seedcorn for *Godot* (Feldman 2015: 119).

Although Beckett is sometimes classed with Ionesco and the early Adamov as an 'absurd' dramatist, the cap has never entirely fitted. If images of isolation, meaninglessness and the breakdown of language are common to the absurdists, Beckett reserves judgement on the first two questions. Finding the universe meaningless would be for Beckett as dogmatic a position as would religious belief or atheism. On language's inability to communicate, his dialogue is a far cry from straightforward endorsement. More accurately stated, he attempted to stretch the possibilities of syntax and lexis to create a theatrical language appropriate to tragicomedy. As Beckett progressively restricts his characters' potential for expansive movement in plays such as *Endgame*, *Happy Days* and *Play*, so minute changes of position and minimal gestures assume disproportionate importance. Linguistically, Beckett imparts to his dialogue a grammar that images their predicaments, revealing aspects of the experience that is at the play's heart. Language carries elements of the metatheatricality that, as we have seen, is a constant aspect of tragicomedy, drawing attention in Beckett's scripts to its own curious properties. When Clov says 'If I don't kill that rat, he'll die' (Beckett [1958] 1973: 44), the grammar plays a trick on us. The sentence poses as a genuine disjunctive of the form 'if not-x, then y', but there is no true juxtaposition of alternatives – or is there? Grammar and syntax have imposed on the passive verb 'to die' an active role appropriate to a Clov's-eye view of experience. To him, dying is the supreme expression of freedom possible in the austere, debilitated world that he and the rat inhabit. Suddenly, dying seems like a glorious expression of malevolent will on the rat's part, the more so because it deprives Clov of an opportunity to act in killing him.

Beckett's celebrated metaphysical jokes are, I am suggesting, the newly minted language of modern tragicomedy. From *Godot*: 'The tears of the world are a constant quantity. For each one who begins to weep, somewhere else another stops. The same is true of the laugh' (Beckett [1956] 1967: 33). As the audience ponders that and begins to giggle, so they must ponder that they may be preventing laughter elsewhere on the globe. 'There's no lack of void' (66), where the negative particle applied to a negative noun 'lack', coupled with another, 'void', adds up to something almost palpably present. From *Endgame*, where Beckett does so much with 'nothing': 'Nothing is funnier than unhappiness, I grant you that' (20); or 'Better than nothing? Is that possible?' (40). Straight man to comic sequences such as 'Clov: Do you believe in the life to come? Hamm: Mine was always that. Got him that time!' (35) seem to involve a kind of linguistic ambush. There can be few dramatists who have achieved more than Beckett by punctuating 'ordinary' discourse with individual words taken from an entirely different linguistic register. In *Godot* alone, the words 'knook' and 'morpion' are found. When the pair try an insult sequence to kill some time, they find from somewhere the terms 'gonococcus' and 'spirochaete'. Examples can be found in every Beckett play that has words. Particularly liberating and remarkable about Beckett characters is that their word-hoard can be so unexpectedly rich, in defiance of what seem to be their class or existential predicaments. Willie in *Happy Days* (1961), a repulsive character who occupies some of his onstage time in rhythmic below-the-waist activities, is still good for the word 'formication' (Beckett [1961] 1973: 24).

Characters as circumstantially challenged as Beckett's, who possess linguistic resources in tension with their overtly narrow horizons, are an important aspect of Beckett's achievement in tragicomedy. It is as if what they lack in psychology, possessing 'memories' entirely discontinuous with their current identities, they make up for in language. Beckett's interest in tragicomedy is a point of difference between his theatre and that of the absurdists. What seems most likely is that in calling *Godot* a tragicomedy, Beckett wished to put future directors and audiences upon notice that it was not to be played either for tears or for laughs: that what was vital to a successful interpretation was an uneasy *balance* created by dialectical tension. In this context, 'balance' does not mean the symmetry encountered in, for example, neoclassical adaptations of Shakespeare such as Tate's *Lear*. Those derive their aesthetic from the security of a paternal, quasi-absolute monarchy, where the King still has some of the trappings of divine sanction and where religious belief, channelled through a national church, is relatively securely in place. Beckett's world is one in which an unimaginably bloody war has been fought to end a toxic form of absolutism, national governments are in tatters and extreme challenges have been posed to any form of religious belief. 'Balance' here refers not to the benign probability implied in Pascal's wager (Blaise Pascal [1623–62] whose idea was that there is more to be gained by believing in God than by not believing) but to a hedged bet, a fifty–fifty chance that there is some meaning to human existence. Here, we refer to the probability patterns produced by a stochastic approach to experience.

Tragicomic form in Beckett, I am arguing, speaks to a metaphysics appropriate to a statistical modern age, an age that calculates probabilities rather than endorses any religious belief. Hinging between bleak and optimistic outcomes, Beckett sometimes plays out this game of chance on the level of the sentence, economizing on effects that in earlier tragicomedy entire scenes have been dedicated to achieving. In Shakespeare's late tragicomedies, the happy ending is mythico-religious, and in Fletcher's, the happy endings testify to the existence of Providence, providing a sense of fate or destiny that sees to it, through coincidences, miraculous interventions – the right people being in the right places at the right time – that the worst consequences of human malice do not eventuate. Piling up chance event upon chance event, the paradoxical effect of Fletcherian plotting is to turn randomness into its opposite, patterned Providence. Beckett's plays examine the chances of there being any source of meaning whatsoever in human life. Take the tree in *Godot* for example. It is positioned somewhere between being a meaningful symbol and a metatheatrical joke at the expense of stage sets for realist plays. Usually in realist dramas, such scenic elements and stage props are practicable: they work. The two protagonists consider hanging themselves from the tree exulting in the prospect that 'it'd give us an erection' (17). But the pair doubt the flimsy tree's capacity to hold their weight. Their weight, however, is, like most personal details in this Alzheimeresque play where what happened yesterday cannot be remembered tomorrow, a fugitive matter: Vladimir: 'But am I heavier than you?' Estragon: 'There's an even chance' (18). Even that is a question of probability. Later, when Estragon tries unsuccessfully to conceal himself behind the tree, Vladimir's disgusted reaction again becomes an aspect of the play's ongoing metatheatrical irony in line with others that have punctuated the action. Vladimir: 'Decidedly this tree will not have been of the slightest use to us' (74).

Another way of putting this point about Beckettian tragicomedy and the 'stochastic' – the domain of probability, odds and random distribution – is to follow up on the well-known crux in Beckett studies centred on Vladimir's 'One of the thieves was saved. (*Pause.*) It's a reasonable percentage' (11). It is sometimes said to refer to an injunction of St Augustine, one that raises the question of balance and odds: 'Do not despair: one of the thieves was saved. Do not presume: one of the thieves was damned.' Such a passage has never been located in Augustine, however, and the more immediate reference is to the account given in the Gospels of the two thieves crucified with Christ. In only one version, that of Luke 22.39–45, the words of a repentant and an unregenerate malefactor are recounted. To the repentant sinner, Christ says 'To day shalt thou be with me in paradise.' Vladimir is fixated on the question of odds. If as he says 'all four were there' (13) – in itself a comical misunderstanding, the idea that all four Evangelists were eye-witnesses of the Crucifixion – why does only one of them record this and, by implication, what does that do to modify the odds on salvation? This emphasis on binary outcomes is resumed at the end of Act 1 when the boy arrives to tell them that Godot won't come that night. We learn that the boy minds the goats for Godot and is treated fairly well, but his brother, who minds the sheep, is beaten. The allusion is to Matthew 25, to Christ's words: 'And before him shall be gathered all nations: and he shall separate them one from another, as a shepherd divideth his sheep from the goats. And he shall set the sheep on his right hand, but the goats on the left' (vv. 32–3). The sheep are to be saved. For postwar European audiences, the procedure might recall the macabre randomness of concentration camp selection. From Estragon, it elicits the unexpected confession that 'All my life I've compared myself to [Christ]' (52).

Beckettian tragicomedy serves the same purpose as tragicomedy was originally devised to serve: to be a dramatic form that represents more adequately the complexity of experience. Post-1945, that complexity resides in the question whether human life has any meaning beyond the fact of its presence on earth, a question renewed by death on an unimaginable scale and inconceivably gratuitous cruelty in recent history. In the foregoing brief analysis, I have tried to show how a bleakly agnostic existential philosophy is held in tandem with a series of self-reflexive jokes about performance; and how Beckett has devised a language that educes comic effects from epistemological cul-de-sacs. Throughout the play, a pessimism so lyrically and creatively expressed as to contain within it a flicker of at least linguistic hope is juxtaposed with a constantly engaging and often hilarious series of surface activities designed to defeat boredom and punctuate time. Does meaning reside in the pessimism of Godot's non-advent, or in the digressions? Pozzo's actorly and superior manner, the difficulty he has even seeing himself as of the same species as Vladimir and Estragon, is suggestive of a sometime tragic protagonist or ancient despot. He and Lucky contribute a series of sadomasochistic actions, to some extent reversed in the second act, that show the arbitrary nature of power but even more the fickleness of human sympathy: Pozzo: 'Remark that I might just as well have been in his shoes and he in mine. If chance had not willed otherwise' (31). The way self-interest combines with humanity, differently balanced in Vladimir than in Estragon, is in itself a profound commentary on the stretch of history recently endured. Estragon being kicked painfully in the shins when he offers to dry Lucky's tears with a handkerchief is a perfect tragicomic moment. Another such occurs at the very end of the play, when Estragon takes off his belt with a view to hanging himself and, circus-clown-like, his trousers fall down. Few dramatists have tried to make us laugh at attempted suicide – though Ibsen was one of the few, as was Chekhov, with his character Yepihodov constantly carrying his revolver and contemplating self-sacrifice.

All the activity in the play, its formidable range of props, its music-hall and circus routines with hat-swapping and pratfalls and its darkly comic song, is subsumed to the logic of *waiting* (Figures 13a and 13b). The characters are in an expectant attitude, expecting something else, something to happen other than what is happening – and by implication more important than what is happening. They await Godot's *advent*. Talk displaces, even *becomes* action. What happens is a displacement activity for what doesn't happen. Yet in this play and in all of Beckett's drama, he does things at the level of lexis and syntax that other dramatists have seldom rivalled. The liveliness of the Beckettian sentence to some extent at least annuls the pessimism of the overarching metaphysic. It seems particularly appropriate that I should be writing this paragraph at a time, during the Covid-19 lockdown period in the UK,

Figure 13a *Rory Nolan (Pozzo), Garrett Lombard (Lucky), Marty Rea (Vladimir) and Aaron Monaghan (Estragon) in an Edinburgh International Festival production of* Waiting for Godot *at the Lyceum Theatre in 2018, directed by Garry Hynes. Photo by Roberto Ricciuti/Getty Images.*

Figure 13b *Ian McKellen (Estragon), Patrick Stewart (Vladimir), Simon Callow (Pozzo)* and *Ronald Pickup (Lucky) in Sean Mathias' production of* Waiting for Godot *at the Theatre Royal, Haymarket in 2009. Photo by robbie jack/Corbis via Getty Images.*

when the entire world and its myriad activities are subsumed to the logic of *waiting*. At the moment, we are all characters in a Beckett play. We are experiencing the peculiar distortion of time where hours appear to be long and weeks short, where we too may be trying to fill in time with routines, schticks and anecdotes. Many of us are trying to do creative things with sentences. I hope this book has occasionally succeeded.

NOTES

Introduction

1 Gerald Baker has generously provided me with lists drawn from multiple sources of plays that have in those sources been termed tragicomedies, as well as finding a list of plays performed post-1660. His work is indebted to Martin Wiggins and Catherine Richardson (2012), as is my own.

2 See Kewes (2004).

Chapter 1

1 Robert Watson is the author of the introduction to the Arden Third Series edition of *Measure for Measure*, co-edited with A. R. Braunmuller (Shakespeare 2020).

Chapter 2

1 See Neill (2007).

Chapter 3

1 Quoted in Georges Forestier's 1988 edition of Corneille's *Le Cid* (Corneille 1988: 10).

2 Robert Hume provides a fuller account: 'Taken in toto, performance records are both sparse and spotty. For the four decades 1660–1700 we know the play and venue for 949 of an estimated 14,067 performances given at patent theatres in London – which is about 6.7%. From custom (three days minimum for a new play if possible), sources like *Roscius Anglicanus*, and comments in prefaces, letters, and other such materials, we may plausibly infer another 1502 performances, which is an additional 10.7%. Or from the perspective of what we do not know, we are clueless as to what was performed on 82.6% of the days on which we have reason to believe a performance occurred in a public theatre' (Hume 2016: sec. VI).

WORKS CITED

Anon. (1690), *The Royal voyage, or, The Irish expedition*, London: Richard Baldwin.

Beaumont, Francis and John Fletcher. (1966–96), *The Dramatic Works in the Beaumont and Fletcher Canon*, ed. Fredson Bowers, 10 vols, Cambridge: Cambridge University Press.

Beaumont, Francis and John Fletcher. (1973), *Philaster*, ed. Andrew Gurr, Manchester: Manchester University Press.

Beaumont, Francis and John Fletcher. (2009), *Philaster*, ed. Suzanne Gossett, London: Methuen.

Beckett, Samuel. ([1956] 1967), *Waiting for Godot*, London: Faber.

Beckett, Samuel. ([1958] 1973), *Endgame*, London: Faber.

Beckett, Samuel. ([1961] 1973), *Happy Days*, London: Faber.

Beckett, Samuel. (1984), *Collected Shorter Plays*, London: Faber.

Boucicault, Dion. (1987), *Selected Plays*, ed. Andrew Parkin, Gerrards Cross: Colin Smythe.

Carlson, Marvin. (1984), *Theories of the Theatre: A Historical and Critical Survey from the Greeks to the Present*, Ithaca, NY: Cornell University Press.

Chapelain, Jean. (1638), *Les Sentimens de l'Académie Françoise sur la tragicomédie du Cid*, Paris: Camusat.

Chekhov, Anton. (1912), *Two Plays by Tchekhof*, ed. and trans. George Calderon, London: Grant Richards.

Chekhov, Anton. ([1951] 1970), *The Cherry Orchard* (1904), in *Plays*, ed. Elizaveta Fen, Harmondsworth: Penguin.

Chekhov, Anton. ([1964] 2008), *Five Plays*, ed. Ronald Hingley, Oxford: Oxford University Press.

Chekhov, Anton. (1974–83), *Complete Works and Letters*, 30 vols, Moscow: Nauka.

Corneille, Pierre. ([1638] 1650), *Le Cid*, trans. Joseph Rutter, 2nd edn., London: Humphrey Moseley.

Corneille, Pierre. (1988), *Le Cid*, ed. Georges Forestier, Paris: Louis Magnard.

Dillon, Janette. (2002), 'Elizabethan Comedy', in Alexander Leggatt (ed.), *The Cambridge Companion to Shakespearean Comedy*, 47–63, Cambridge: Cambridge University Press.

Drummond, William of Hawthornden. (1623), *Flowres of Sion ... to which is adioned his Cypresse grove*, Edinburgh: A. Hart.

Dryden, John. (1664), *The Rival Ladies*, London: Herringman.

Dryden, John. (1669), *Secret-Love, or, The Maiden-Queen*, London: Herringman.

Dryden, John. (1681), *The Spanish Fryar, or, the Double-Discovery*, London: Richard and Jacob Tonson.

Dryden, John. (1971), 'Of Dramatick Poesy' (1668), in *Of Dramatic Poesy and other Critical Essays*, 2 vols, ed. George Watson, London: Dent.

Dryden, John. (1978), *Marriage à la Mode* (1671), in *Dryden: A Selection*, ed. John Conaghan, London: Methuen.

Duncan-Jones, Katherine. (2001), *Ungentle Shakespeare: Scenes from His Life*, London: Arden Shakespeare.

Dürrenmatt, Friedrich. (1962), *The Visit*, trans. Patrick Bowles, London: Cape.

Edwards, Philip and Colin Gibson, eds. (1976), *The Plays and Poems of Philip Massinger*, 5 vols, Oxford: Clarendon Press.

Feldman, Matthew. (2015), *Falsifying Beckett: Essays on Archives, Philosophy and Methodology in Beckett Studies*, Stuttgart: Ibidem.

Fenton, James. (2016), *Don Quixote: A Play with Songs Adapted from the Novel by Miguel de Cervantes*, London: Faber.

Fletcher, John. (1610), *The Faithfull Shepheardess*, London: By Edward Allde for R. Bonian and H. Walley.

Fletcher, John. (2017), *The Island Princess*, ed. Clare McManus, London: Bloomsbury.

Foster, Verna A. (2004), *The Name and Nature of Tragicomedy*, Aldershot: Ashgate.

Fowler, Alastair. (1985), *Kinds of Literature: An Introduction to the Theory of Genres and Modes*, Oxford: Clarendon Press.

Gay, John. (1983), *The What D'Ye Call It: a Tragi-Comi-Pastoral Farce* (1715), in *John Gay. Dramatic Works*, ed. John Fuller, 2 vols, Oxford: Clarendon Press.

Guarini, Giovanni Battista. (1602), *Il Pastor Fido: or The Faithfull Shepheard*, London: Printed for Simon Waterson.

Guarini, Giovanni Battista. (1914), *Il Pastor Fido e Il Compendio della Poesia Tragicomica, a cura di Gioachino Brognoligo*, Bari: Gius, Laterza e Figli.

Gurr, Andrew. (2004), *The Shakespeare Company 1594–1642*, Cambridge: Cambridge University Press.

Habermas, Jürgen. (1989), *The Structural Transformation of the Public Sphere* (1962), trans. Thomas Burger with Frederick Lawrence, Cambridge, MA: MIT Press.

Hammond, Brean, ed. (2010), *Double Falsehood*, London: Methuen.

Hammond, Brean and Shaun Regan. (2006), *Making the Novel: Fiction and Society in Britain, 1660–1789*, Basingstoke: Palgrave Macmillan.

Hédelin, François, abbé d'Aubignac (1684), *La pratique du théâtre* (1657), trans. as *The whole art of the stage*, London: Cadman, Bentley, Smith and Fox.

Heywood, Thomas. (1633), *The English Traveller*, London: Printed by Robert Raworth.

Howard, Sir Robert. (1665), *Four New Plays*, London: Herringman.

Hume, Robert D. (2016), 'Theatre Performance Records in London, 1660–1705', *Review of English Studies*, 67.280 (June): 468–95.

Ibsen, Henrik. ([1950] 1965), *The Wild Duck* (1884), in *Hedda Gabler and Other Plays*, trans. Una Ellis-Fermor, Harmondsworth: Penguin.

Ibsen, Henrik. (1980), *The Wild Duck* (1884), in *Ibsen: Plays One*, trans. Michael Meyer, London: Bloomsbury Publishing. Available online: http://dx.doi.org/10.5040/9781408168257.00000004.

Ibsen, Henrik. (2005), *The Wild Duck* (1884), trans. David Eldridge, London: Bloomsbury Publishing.

Ionesco, Eugene. (1964), *Notes and Counter Notes*, trans. Donald Watson, London: John Calder.

Kenner, Hugh. (1973), *A Reader's Guide to Samuel Beckett*, New York: Farrar, Straus and Giroux.

Kewes, P. (2004), 'Langbaine, Gerard (1656–1692), Dramatic Cataloguer and Writer', in *Oxford Dictionary of National Biography*. Available online: https://www-oxforddnb-com.ezproxy.nottingham.ac.uk/view/10.1093/ref:odnb/9780198614128.001.0001/odnb-9780198614128-e-16007 (accessed 3 June 2020)

Knowlson, James (1996), *Damned to Fame: The Life of Samuel Beckett*, London: Bloomsbury.

McDonald, Russ. (2006), *Shakespeare's Late Style*, Cambridge: Cambridge University Press.

McFarlane, James. (1970), *Henrik Ibsen*, Penguin Critical Anthologies, Harmondsworth: Penguin.

McInnis, David and Matthew Steggle, eds. (2014), *Lost Plays in Shakespeare's England*, Basingstoke: Palgrave Macmillan.

Marston, John. (1975), *The Malcontent*, ed. G. K. Hunter, London: Methuen.

Meyerhold, Vsevolod Emilyevich. (1968), *Statii, Pisma, Riechi, Besiedy 1891–1917*, Moscow: Iskusstvo.

Middleton, Thomas. (2007), *Thomas Middleton: The Collected Works and Companion*, ed. Gary Taylor and John Lavagnino, Oxford: Oxford University Press.

Milton, John. (1968), *The Poems of John Milton*, ed. John Carey and Alastair Fowler, London: Longmans.

Neill, Michael. (2007), 'Ford, John (bap. 1586, d. 1639×53?), Playwright', in *Oxford Dictionary of National Biography*, 4 October. Available online: https://www-oxforddnb-com.ezproxy.nottingham.ac.uk/view/10.1093/ref:odnb/9780198614128.001.0001/odnb-9780198614128-e-9861 (accessed 7 January 2021)

Nevitt, Marcus and Tanya Pollard, eds. (2019), *Reader in Tragedy: An Anthology of Classical Criticism to Contemporary Theory*, London: Methuen.

Philips, John. (1715), *The earl of Mar marr'd. with the humours of Jockey, the Highlander: a tragi-comical farce*, London: Edmund Curll.

Plautus, Titus Maccius. (1977), *The Rope and Other Plays*, trans. E. F. Watling, Harmondsworth: Penguin.

Potter, Lois. (2012), *The Life of William Shakespeare: A Critical Biography*, Malden, MA: Wiley-Blackwell.

Randall, Dale B. J. and Jackson Campbell Boswell. (2009), *Cervantes in Seventeenth-century England the Tapestry Turned*, Oxford: Oxford University Press.

Rowley, William, Thomas Dekker and John Ford. (1999), *The Witch of Edmonton*, ed. Peter Corbin and Douglas Sedge, Manchester: Manchester University Press.

Samson, Alexander. (2009), '"Last thought upon a Windmill": Cervantes and Fletcher', in J. A. G. Ardila (ed.), *The Cervantean Heritage: Reception and Influence of Cervantes in Britain*, 223–33, Leeds: Legenda.

Schopenhauer, Arthur. (1966), *The World As Will and Representation*, 2 vols, trans. E. F. J. Payne, New York: Dover Press.

Scott, Sir Walter. (1808), *The Works of John Dryden*, 18 vols, London: William Miller.

Shakespeare, William. (1991), *Measure for Measure*, ed. Brian Gibbons, Cambridge: Cambridge University Press.

Shakespeare, William. (2006), *Much Ado About Nothing*, ed. Claire McEachern, London: Arden Shakespeare.

Shakespeare, William (2007), *Hamlet: The Text of 1603 and 1623*, ed. Ann Thompson and Neil Taylor, London: Arden Shakespeare.

Shakespeare, William. (2010), *The Winter's Tale*, ed. John Pitcher, London: Arden Shakespeare.

Shakespeare, William. (2015), *Macbeth*, ed. Sandra Clark and Pamela Mason, London: Arden Shakespeare.

Shakespeare, William. (2017), *Cymbeline*, ed. Valerie Wayne, London: Arden Shakespeare.

Shakespeare, William. (2019), *All's Well That Ends Well*, ed. Suzanne Gossett and Helen Wilcox, London: Arden Shakespeare.

Shakespeare, William. (2020), *Measure for Measure*, ed. A. R. Braunmuller and Robert N. Watson, London: Arden Shakespeare.

Shaw, George Bernard. ([1932] 1948), *The Quintessence of Ibsenism*, in *Major Critical Essays*, London: Constable.

Shelton, Thomas. (1612), *The History of the Valorous and Witty Knight Errant, Don Quixote of the Mancha. Translated out of the Spanish. The first part*, London: Printed for Ed: Blounte.

Sidney, Sir Philip. (2004), *Sidney's 'The Defence of Poesy' and Selected Renaissance Literary Criticism*, ed. Gavin Alexander, London: Penguin.

Southerne, Thomas. (1988), *The Fatal Marriage; or, the Innocent Adultery* (1694), in *The Works of Thomas Southerne*, ed. Robert Jordan and Harold Love, 2 vols, Oxford: Clarendon Press.

Southerne, Thomas. (1995), *The Wives Excuse* (1692), in *Four Restoration Marriage Plays*, ed. Michael Cordner with Ronald Clayton, Oxford: Oxford University Press.

Stanislavski, Konstantin Sergeievich (1984), *A.P. Chekhov's Correspondence*, Moscow: Khudozhestvennaya Literatura.

Strindberg, August. (1976), *Miss Julie* (1888), trans. Michael Meyer, London: Methuen.

Styan, John Louis. (1978), *Chekhov in Performance: A Commentary on the Major Plays*, Cambridge: Cambridge University Press.
Tate, Nahum. (1681), *The History of King Lear*, London: R. Bentley and M. Magnes.
Tate, Nahum. (1687), *The Island-Princess*, London: W. Canning.
Van Es, Bart. (2013), *Shakespeare in Company*, Oxford: Oxford University Press.
Van Hulle, Dirk and Pim Verhulst. (2017), *The Making of Samuel Beckett's En attendant Godot/Waiting for Godot*, London: Bloomsbury.
Vega, Lope Félix de. (1609), *Arte nuevo de hacer comedias en este tiempo*.
Villiers, George, Duke of Buckingham (1976), *The Rehearsal* (1671), ed. D. E. L. Crane, Durham: University of Durham.
Wayne, Valerie. (2012), '*Don Quixote* and Shakespeare's Collaborative Turn to Romance', in David Carnegie and Gary Taylor (eds.), *The Quest for Cardenio: Shakespeare, Fletcher, Cervantes, and the Lost Play*, 217–38, Oxford: Oxford University Press.
Whetstone, George. (1584), *A Mirour for Magestrates of Cyties*, London: Richard Jones.
Wiggins, Martin and Catherine Richardson. (2012), *British Drama 1533–1642: A Catalogue*, 11 vols, New York: Oxford University Press.

INDEX